IN THE FOOTSTEPS OF
GLORY

TIMOTHY H. GOAD SR.

DEDICATION

I dedicate this book to God and the Holy Spirit, for giving me the opportunity and insight to put down on paper a compelling look at what might have been going through the minds and hearts of the men who formed our Christian heritage as they walked side by side with our Lord Jesus Christ.

I am also dedicating this book to my Mother and Father for all the sacrifices they endured during their lives in order that my brothers and sister, along with myself, had every opportunity to pursue and achieve anything we dreamed. My only regret is taking some fifty five years to let them know how much I really appreciated everything they did to make sure we never did without.

With Love,
Timothy Hadley Goad Sr.

CHAPTER 1

I T WAS A DAY NOT unlike many thousands I had endured. The weather was hot and sweltering, bordering on the cusp of miserable, which was exactly what you would expect from this region in early summer. A half-hearted breeze rustled the sails, kicking up a light chop on the usually tranquil sea.

We were in earlier than usual, having little to show for a long night's work except tired and aching hands, revealing signs of being hard and crusted from many years of pulling rough ropes and nets in the relentless sun.

Andrew, my brother who was two years my junior, was an exceptional fisherman. Being well skilled, he could handle the boat in every situation and find fish in the dark of night. What he lacked in size could be measured in heart and determination. This life we chose—or more accurately, this life that chose us by birth—had served our families well for generations, but it was work in every sense of the word.

"How did you do," questioned John from a nearby boat.

"Not well," I shot back, with no attempt to disguise my disgust. "We would have done better at the market."

"I know the feeling," John's brother, James, chimed in, his words nearly lost in a sudden gust of wind. With a look of embarrassment, the two exhausted men displayed their long night's take, four meager fish.

"If it makes you feel any better, you bested Andrew and me by two."

"We'd better stop this chitchat and get these boats beached. I feel a storm coming," Andrew barked. If my brother sounded the alarm on bad weather, you could write it down in stone, it was coming.

John and James worked with their father on the same boat where my father had learned his trade many years ago. When my father died unexpectedly at a relatively young age, I was left with the burden of growing up quickly, taking care of my mother and helping with my two younger brothers. Looking back, I can clearly see the good that came from what I thought to be tragedy at the time. While I longed to play with the other boys my age, when it came time for them to grow up, I was years ahead of them, and already seasoned in the vocation that would be the fate of most young men living on this lake shore.

As we worked to beach the boats, securing them against any storm surge, little did I know that this day would change my life forever.

<hr/>

Off in the distance a solitary figure made his way toward us. As he neared I could see he was a man in his late twenties, maybe thirty, and definitely not from around here. When you spend your life in a small town, you get to know everyone and their business. Like it or not, it's just that way.

The man called to me in a voice that begged for me to listen.

"How was the catch?"

"A night of futile effort, I'm afraid. Dismal by anyone's standards," I answered, continuing to tug on the boat.

As my brother and I toiled, safely securing our boat for the night, I was suddenly overcome with the sensation that this stranger had something on his mind that was much more important than our day's catch. He was a lean fellow, with a complexion that let me know he had spent a little time in the sun. Nevertheless, nothing about him prompted me to think he had ever done any fishing. Fishermen always seem to have a squint in their eyes and hands that give them away, even without a handshake.

Then, as if brought forth from the sand, a large crowd appeared from over the rise of the lake bank. Apparently they had been following the stranger, and they began begging him to teach.

Teach what? And why on the banks of this sea? Has this man no other place to teach? Must he come out to where I work and disrupt my simple way of life?

The crowd continued to press in, as if mesmerized by what this man had been saying. What could he be teaching that would have so many people hungering for his words as if they were starving dogs? He is most likely another prophet, offering some vision of hope for our people. Most Jews would grasp at any promise of freedom from another generation of Roman occupation and dominance.

Are we really God's chosen people? Chosen for what, the humiliation and amusement of Rome? Watching and seeing, I sometimes wonder if our own leaders, political and religious alike, aren't in it for their personal welfare, selling out their very own flesh and blood for a life of prominence, power and comfort.

I do believe the God of our fathers has a very different plan than the one I see unfolding, a plan that releases us from the tyranny and grip of such a ruthless nation, but when?

The news of a great messiah has been preached by prophets and taught to us for centuries. Still, generations have come and gone and nothing has changed.

As I gazed into the crowd, lost in my thoughts of hopes to come, I was shaken back into the moment by Andrew.

"Simon," Andrew said, with some urgency in his voice. "The stranger has asked to board our boat and push out a short distance in order that he may teach."

"What is it that he is teaching?" I asked a stranger in the crowd.

"The good news of the kingdom!" he replied with an enthusiasm that was rare in these harsh times.

"I could use some good news about now," I said to my brother, "Let's push out with this teacher and see what all the fuss is about."

The light chop on the lake posed no challenge to an experienced fisherman, but I suspected it might make a rough platform for teaching. Amazingly, the instant the teacher climbed aboard the wind subsided, making the sea calm and allowing every word to be clearly heard. As we pushed off from the shore a short distance, leaving the crowd on the shoreline, I could hear murmurs circulating about healings this man had performed. If the accounts were true, that certainly would put this teacher at a different level then others I had heard.

As he spoke, my heart felt as though it had been touched. His words were more than idle talk and scriptural rhetoric, transcending everyday scripture lessons. The large crowd gathered on the shore was as quiet as death itself, transfixed on this prophetic stranger. His face radiated as he delivered his compelling truths, removing any doubt, in my mind at least, that he truly believed everything he taught.

I can't tell you how long this went on. Time seemed to vanish, but nevertheless, it did end, and there we were some fifty yards from shore.

"Where are you from? I've never seen you about this town," Andrew straightened up and asked. The teacher stared at the water for what seemed like minutes, as if no question had been asked, then he calmly pointed out into the sea and said, "There, put out your nets for a catch."

Although I had a genuine admiration for this man and his teaching, what I said next came out on its own, as if my mouth had been separated from my mind.

"My friend, I can't for the life of me, understand how you could possibly expect us to do such a foolish thing. It is apparent that you're not a man of the sea, much less a fisherman. We have worked all night and into the morning, with only two fish to show for our efforts. I'm exhausted, fatigued and hungry, and now a man I've never met is telling me to take my boat back into the deeper water for a catch. With the utmost respect for you as a teacher or prophet, a fisherman you are not, sir. Furthermore, I resent the implication that you know where to find the fish and that men who have done this their entire lives don't. We know this sea like the back of our hands. We've been fishing it for thirty-two years, quite successfully, I might add. If there were fish to catch, they'd be in the boat!"

Unwavering and with a gentle smile, as if I had said nothing, he pointed and made the same request. "There, put out your nets for a catch."

Grabbing Andrew by the shoulder I turned him around and snarled under my breath, "What could this man possibly know?"

"I can't begin to know," he muttered. "But looking over our catch, my guess is the same could be asked of us." His eyes met mine as he shrugged his shoulders. "What could we possibly have to lose? Heaven knows we could use some good luck."

With that, the anchor was retrieved and we headed for deeper water.

When we reached the area pointed out by the man we now knew to be Jesus from Nazareth, we were instructed to lower the nets. In all my years of fishing, I can't recall a time when I had been more reluctant to lower my nets, but to satisfy this teacher's request and my eagerness to prove him wrong, down they went.

Within moments the nets were pulled from our hands with such force that the entire boat lurched and changed direction. The water began to boil with fish and immediately I knew the catch was much bigger than Andrew and I could handle.

John and his brother were still sitting on their boat at the shore, watching to see how this new fishing guide would do.

"Bring your boat quickly," I shouted. "Our nets are at the breaking point and the boat will never handle this catch!"

In an instant they were in the water and headed in our direction. When they pulled alongside us, their faces told the story.

"I've never seen a catch like this in all my life!" yelled James.

Although I had quite a few years of age and experience on James, I could have said the same thing.

After struggling for what seemed like hours, we managed between the two boats and four men to get our catch to the beach. The large crowd that had assembled to listen to Jesus was buzzing about the unbelievable catch we had just hauled to shore.

As we sent some young boys for more baskets to carry the fish, several cries of "It's a miracle!" could be heard rising from the crowd.

While this was the largest catch any of us had ever seen, I didn't know if it fell into the miracle category or not. I didn't ever remember witnessing a miracle, but if the stories that this crowd were telling about this Jesus healing the sick of every ill imaginable were indeed true, then maybe, just maybe, I had seen my first.

The youngsters returned with the baskets, and we began to fill them. I could not believe my eyes, but there in front of me stood twelve full baskets of fish, each holding over one hundred fish. My only thought was that if this Jesus were to stay on with us, our fishing business would be like no other. Little did I know that this moment, which had me delirious with expectation of things to come, would mark the last catch I would make for years.

The news of the catch had reached the town and hundreds of people began showing up, not only to see the catch but to put their eyes on this new prophet, or as some were calling him, "the Messiah." It was amazing how fast a crowd of people could anoint someone to the status of Messiah, which requires that one be sent from God himself.

Then again, if this Jesus had done everything these people said he had done, who was I to say he wasn't?

Before I had a chance to get over all the excitement, Jesus commanded Andrew and me to leave our boat and nets and follow him. He said, "I will make you fishers of men."

Fishers of men? What in the world was this man talking about? This was the only life I knew.

However, his command which should have been unsettling, seemed to answer a question somewhere deep within me, and I knew I had to go with him. It was as though the darkness had been lifted, and I could see. I called him Lord, and begged him to leave me, for I was a sinful man. He only smiled and said, come.

He headed in the direction of John and James,

who were busy mending their nets, which had broken with the great harvest of fish and making ready their share of the catch for a trip to the market.

The owner of the boat was their father, a man named Zebedee, who in past years had spent countless time fishing with my father, the two learning their trade by trial and error. As my mind shifted back in time, I could see us sitting on our boats as Zebedee revisited his past, telling us of the time he had fallen overboard in a violent storm, and my father, despite not being the greatest of swimmers, dove in with a rope and saved his life.

He said, "Your father was no fool. He had lashed himself to the boat with what he thought was enough rope and in he came."

I loved the man they called Zebedee. He had stood in as a father after ours had passed away. Now, I knew what was coming his way, and I didn't know how he would take it.

Jesus wasted no time in asking John and James to lay down their nets and follow him. For a moment neither brother knew how to answer his invitation. Seeing their agony at the realization that following Jesus meant walking away from their father was tearing a hole in my heart. Jesus knew exactly what was coursing through both men, so we continued along the beach, giving the two brothers a moment of private time to say their farewells.

Who could have imagined what had transpired in the space of a few hours. I couldn't wrap my head around it, nor did I want to look into the future because for the first time in my life I seemed to be out of control. I was walking away from the only thing I knew how to do in order to follow a man some believed to be the Messiah. Where I was going, I had no idea.

I did know this: Despite this sudden and drastic upheaval in my life, I had never experienced such a calming peace.

CHAPTER 2

THIS MAN JESUS POSSESSED A remarkable ability to make me feel at ease. He seemed to know me better than my own brother, and I found peace just being in his presence. I knew my life had changed forever, and I only hoped that whatever Jesus expected from me, I could deliver.

He spoke like no one I had ever heard. He had wisdom beyond comprehension and the ability to soften the hardest heart. What could he possibly need from a grizzled fisherman like me, or any of us for that matter? All four of us had spent our entire lives catching fish, never leaving the town of Bethsaida, except for the annual trip to Jerusalem. Yet, we followed Jesus along that shore without knowing our destination. I wondered if Jesus himself knew where the journey would end.

But those questions did not trouble me; the answers Jesus had for much larger questions were more important.

As we walked, thoughts of what I had left behind raced along with dreams of what was to come, both fighting for equal time. What I left behind I had known for many years, but the promise and hope that flowed from the fountain of Jesus' words took years off my stride. It was comforting to know my brother and two close fishing friends were also on this journey, so if we failed at catching men, there was always the Sea of Galilee. But failure was not something I accepted, nor did I have any intention of letting this man down.

He made his way to that beach with the knowledge, or at least the hope, that we would answer his call. Among the crowd following Jesus were people from many different areas and walks of life. I wondered how so many folks could just drop what they were doing and follow a man from town to town, without a plan or money. Then I realized I was talking about myself as well. It wasn't hard to figure out how it happened; just listening to Jesus talk for a short time could set the hook.

It was the constant banging in my head, "Why me?" that left me blank. If you asked someone from our town, "Tell me, can you name the holy men and people of faith living in this city," I can assure you my name would not be on the list. It's not that I am not a religious man, I am. It's just that the holy law always seemed to be something for the Sabbath, not for the rest of the week. I was more likely to damn the fish and curse the weather than to tell someone about the kingdom of God.

So, why me?

Suddenly, from out of the crowd, something burst through the mass of humanity and cowered at the teacher's feet. It was a man, covered with a skin disease, the likes of which I had not seen since passing near the city of lepers. Immediately the stench of rotting flesh and filthy bandages filled the air, causing the people near him to cover their noses in an attempt to filter out the almost unbearable odor.

"Get him away from here before he infects us all!" they shouted, as the men closest to him started to drag the man away by his feet. I was in agreement with the crowd, if for no other reason than to clear the air of the awful smell.

Anguished eyes looked up from a grotesque face as the poor man cried out to Jesus, "You can heal me if you want! Please, make me clean!"

Instead of recoiling in horror at the possibility of catching this contagious disease, Jesus reached out and touched the disfigured man and said, "I do want to. Be clean."

In that instant the disease was gone. The sores vanished. Skin that had been decaying was now smooth and whole. The man was indeed clean.

There were gasps from the crowd, but not the wild commotion I would have expected. Many of the people had been following Jesus for quite some time and had seen him heal many times. But for myself, I lost the strength in my legs and fell to my knees—exactly where I belonged, I thought. I looked over at Andrew, James and John. No words were needed. Their faces said it all.

The amazing fish catch had surpassed anything we had ever seen. Still, in the backs of our minds, we all knew it could have been an unbelievably lucky guess, or maybe a blessing from God on His own accord. But now, right before our eyes, a man had been miraculously cleansed of an incurable disease, and it was this man Jesus who had said, "Be clean."

CHAPTER 3

J ESUS TOLD THE MAN NOT to tell anyone what had taken place, but to go and show himself to the priest, then do as Moses had ordered and make a sacrifice to show that he was cured. I know the man left us with that intention, but he didn't do what he was ordered to do. Instead he went into the nearby towns telling everyone who would listen about the good thing Jesus had done for him. Not that I fault him—I am not sure I could have kept quiet if I had been in his shoes—but it wasn't long before I knew why Jesus had told the man to keep the miracle to himself.

How could news spread so fast? The crowds grew threefold in the span of a day, and the clamor from so many people wanting to be heard was deafening. Quiet conversations with Jesus were impossible; he was healing people from the rising sun to sundown, with hardly any time to lay down his head. However, he always made time to withdraw from the crowd and us to pray. Countless times each day I thought to myself, this man they call Jesus is truly amazing.

There were so many people who heard of Jesus and the miracles he was performing that going into a town was often out of the question. We stayed on the outskirts of towns and villages and did nothing to call attention to ourselves, but the crowds were like tracking dogs. They found us no matter what.

Years of fishing had kept me in good shape, and I had no health problems to speak of, so maybe that is why I had little patience for the constant cries, day and night, of "Heal me, Jesus! Help me, Jesus! I want to be well, Jesus!" It's not that I lacked compassion or understanding—I am quite certain if I were afflicted with any of these diseases or handicaps, I would be on the front row calling out his name—it's just that I longed for the peaceful sunrises on my boat, a gentle breeze in my face and only an occasional seabird calling to me for a handout. My time with Jesus can still be measured in days, but already the peaceful solitude I once knew, in contrast to the roar of an ever-growing sea of humanity, is almost more than I can bear.

However, just as I began to feel my limits being stretched and the walls closing in, Jesus stopped the madness of this new spinning world by sitting us down and began to teach, taking Andrew, James, John and me away from the crowds to pray and fill us with his marvelous words. His sense of timing for these things was perfect. It is as if he were in my heart and mind, a musician knowing exactly when his instrument was in need of tuning.

I worry for Jesus. What must this be doing to him? If indeed he is bothered or unnerved by the pressure of the crowds, it never shows. He is always smiling and compassionate in the face of the never-ending deluge of requests for his time. He never begrudges the many times they walk away ungrateful. Why would any man subject himself to such a life? This is a question I intend to ask him if I am ever permitted a quiet moment and he is not too tired to tell me.

We made our way back to Capernaum, where Jesus had been invited to a follower's home to teach. The news of Jesus being there spread like wildfire and it wasn't long before the crowd began pressing to hear him, filled the house and spilled outside the structure.

As Jesus taught and preached the message, I couldn't help but notice some of the teachers of the law were present. With this lot you never knew where you stood, and I wondered what it was they were there to hear. The truth in the words of Jesus, one could hope, but probably not. I kept an eye on them, fearing they would make their presence known before the evening drew to a close.

Something was happening outside the house. The shouts of annoyed and irritated people were making their way inside, and we could hear the sounds of many people on the roof. I knew that people would do anything to get to Jesus, but I was not prepared for what happened next.

With a shower of dust and debris, the roof suddenly opened directly above where Jesus was preaching. I leapt to my feet, thinking something bad was about to happen. But the faces that peered through the hole they had made in the roof were filled with hope, not anger, and four men began to lower a pallet bearing a paralytic man. The man's legs and feet were twisted and drawn up, just skin and bones from lack of use. The crowd was so thick the men couldn't get him in through the door, so they had improvised by getting him to Jesus the only way possible, from above.

I was awestruck by the image. The noonday sun streamed through the hole in the roof, illuminating Jesus with a heavenly glow. His face beamed with pleasure, knowing the kind of faith these men must possess to go through so much trouble for their friend.

Our Lord looked at the motionless man before him and said, "My son, your sins are forgiven."

With an intake of breath that was almost a hiss, the teachers of the law began to squirm and murmur among themselves, "This is blasphemy, God alone forgives sin."

As if he knew their whispered thoughts, Jesus addressed them.

"Why do you murmur among yourselves and think such evil thoughts? Is it easier to say 'Your sins are forgiven you' or 'Stand up and walk?' But so that you may know, I will prove that the Son of Man has authority to forgive sins on earth."

Jesus looked down at the frightened man and said, "Get up and walk. Take your mat and go home."

Immediately the paralyzed man got to his feet and hurried off through the crowd toward the door. I don't recall a "thank you."

To say one miraculous deed is superior to another probably doesn't make sense, but I am here to tell you, everyone who was in that room and saw the same thing I did left with a look I had never seen. It was as if the sun that streamed through that hole in the roof let a little light on each face.

The room was full of praises to God and men

claiming that only God could do such things. The teachers of the law were rethinking their earlier positions, trying to make sense of what they had just witnessed, so I took this opportunity to be the teacher and told them, "It is quite simple, he is the Lord, the long-awaited Messiah."

CHAPTER 4

ON OUR WAY TOWARD THE edge of town, we passed the post of a tax collector named Levi. Like most tax collectors, Levi was a Jew, doing business for personal profit with the Roman government. To other Jews, tax collectors were the lowest form of life, even lower than the Romans, because they stole from their own. Their job consisted of collecting what you owed Rome, and anything above that figure that they could extort went into their pockets. Believe me when I say that a prostitute, beggar or thief was more welcome than one of these vermin.

While I was thinking of these things, I began to become enraged. Surprisingly, Jesus walked over to the tax man and asked him to leave his post and follow him.

Wait a minute, how could such a holy man ask a *tax collector* to join us? Surely Jesus is familiar with the system and how these traitors line their purses with the money they steal from us, their own people. How will this look to the Pharisees and high priests, who are surely watching this new prophet and his followers? They already question Jesus every chance they get, only to find his truths and teachings supported by the same holy words they profess to follow, leaving them to mutter among themselves. They remind me of lions moving along with a herd of animals, staying a safe distance so as not to alarm their prey, while always looking for that single, weakest member, eager to take him out and devour him.

They listen with jackal ears to every word he says, dissecting each syllable and looking for the smallest infraction of the law, as if they were trial lawyers preparing a case.

If these stiff-necked hypocrites would spend as much time listening to Jesus' words of love, life and repentance with a teachable spirit, it would serve them well. Instead, they watch and listen to condemn, not to learn. Their negative presence is a constant threat to our freedom to move about and enable Jesus to spread the good news. If a tax collector is added to the fold, eyebrows will raise and questions are bound to come.

While I was sorting all this out in my mind, we headed for Levi's house, where apparently we would be dining with his family, other tax collectors and a multitude of social outcasts. Had Jesus truly stepped across the line? I mentally began to brace for an onslaught of questions that I surely hoped he could answer.

We had not been there long when just as I predicted, some of the Pharisees started questioning the four of us and the others, asking, "Why does he eat with the likes of these sinners?"

I was not exactly sure how to answer, but I wasn't given the opportunity. Jesus, overhearing their questions, stood up and addressed them.

"What need is there to send a physician to a man who is well? It is a sick man who needs the healing. I have not come to call the righteous, but the sinner to repentance."

What an answer. The Pharisees stood speechless, unable to mount a threat.

Still, I couldn't shake my sense of unease, knowing they would be as relentless as jackals, refusing to accept Jesus as the Messiah that had been prophesied about. For the common man, such as myself, it was as plain as the nose on my face that no one could perform the miracles we had witnessed unless the God of the universe gave him the power to do so. Not so for the scribes, Pharisees and high priests, who, with their superior knowledge of the scriptures, should have been able to spot the Messiah a mile off. It was obvious that they did not want to acknowledge the possibility that Jesus was the anointed one sent from God.

CHAPTER 5

As we continued to move from town to town across the countryside, Jesus continued to add disciples until there were twelve us, whom he called apostles. Was it a coincidence that there were twelve of us and twelve tribes of Israel? I don't know, but I also recalled there were twelve baskets of fish the day that Jesus called us to follow him and be fishers of men.

Time and time again, I told myself I would ask the teacher these questions, but I never did.

Our journey was basically the same from day to day, with Jesus stopping at synagogues and other places that could accommodate large crowds. While there he would teach and heal people, from the poor and outcast to Roman centurions.

A few instances stand out in my mind.

Once, as we were moving through the countryside, the crowds of people were pressing in on us, making our forward progress slow at best. Through the sea of bodies and faces came a man, literally fighting his way to Jesus. He fell on his knees, begging and saying to Jesus, "My little daughter is very sick. Please, come and place your hands on her, so that she may be well and live!"

At once Jesus helped the man to his feet, and we

began to head in the direction from which he had come. I had seen this man before; he was an official at the local synagogue where Jesus had preached the word. I hadn't noticed his position on Jesus and his teachings when we were in his synagogue, but it was obvious he believed, whether through faith in Jesus or the fear of his desperate situation. How sad if it were the latter.

Changing our direction was difficult amidst the crush of people jostling for positions near Jesus. It was always like this—crowding, pushing, arms reaching, and voices pleading for attention or healing. It was controlled pandemonium at best, which is why what happened next was simply astounding. In the midst of all the chaos, Jesus suddenly wheeled around and asked, "Who touched me?"

I thought, who touched you? Are you serious? Any number of about forty different people could have been guilty of touching him at that moment. All of us turned to him with expressions that begged for an explanation for asking such a question.

Again he asked, "Who touched my clothes?"

A woman stepped forward with a look on her face that told everyone she knew exactly what Jesus meant. The crowd quieted and she began to explain.

"I have been afflicted with hemorrhages for twelve years," she said through tears. "The doctors have had no success in healing me, but I thought if only I could touch your cloak, I would be healed. The instant I touched you, the blood flow dried up."

"Daughter, your faith has healed you," Jesus said. "Go in peace and be healed of your trouble."

I had trouble grasping the fact that Jesus had

felt the healing power go out of his body to a woman who touched only the hem of his garment amid a jostling crowd. But there was no time to wonder; the desperate father was hurrying us toward his sick child.

As we continued toward the man's house, one of his servants came running, and it was apparent he was quite distraught. He said there was no need to trouble the teacher any longer, because the man's daughter had passed away.

Acting as if nothing had been said, Jesus told the official, "Don't be afraid, but only believe." He told the crowd that was gathered to remain outside, taking James and John and me into the house. There we were met with the cries and wailing of the sorrowed family and friends.

"Why all this weeping and crying," Jesus asked. "The child is not dead, but only asleep."

Immediately some of the mourners began to ridicule Jesus, saying, "Does this foolish man think we do not know when someone is dead? How dare he come into this man's house at such a time of grief and give him false hope!"

Jesus put them all out of the house, then he took the child's parents and the three of us into the room where she lay. He took the young child's hand and said, "Little girl, I say to you, arise!"

Immediately she opened her eyes and sat up. Getting to her feet, she walked around. Her father and mother were dumbfounded, as were the three of us. Jesus told the parents to tell no one of the miracle and to give the child something to eat.

According to her family, the child was twelve years

old. So, the number twelve has showed up twice more: the woman Jesus healed had hemorrhaged for twelve years, and now this little girl he raised from the dead was twelve. Since I am not a physician I can't say if she was really dead or maybe in a death-like coma. Either way, he commanded her to get up, and she did. That makes what just happened miraculous.

The number twelve simply can't be a coincidence I thought, but then again it was nowhere near as important as what had taken place. Jesus had healed so many people of so many illnesses, but had he just raised someone from the dead? If so, this was something that no magician could do, and I am not sure if any of the prophets of the past ever accomplished such a feat.

The world was his stage; his power was unmatched. Had we truly received our long-awaited Messiah? Was the Roman occupation soon going to become a thing of the past? As we sat around the dying fire, with the glow of the smoldering embers lighting our faces, a small group of us tossed these ideas about. We weren't sure if Jesus shared our feelings or if he had a different plan.

While we solved the problems of the Jewish nation, Jesus was fast asleep, getting some well-needed rest.

I could not get the questions out of my head, even while he slept. I had the feeling he was right in the middle of our conversation, listening and wanting us to ask the questions aloud, the ones it seemed only he could answer. However, except for Matthew, who was good with numbers, there wasn't a scholar among us, especially when it came to scripture. And with all the Pharisees giving it their best shot and falling on their faces, we were smart enough not to put ourselves in that position. Jesus was the only man I had ever seen who never stumbled over a question and always managed to leave the person who asked it questioning himself.

CHAPTER 6

IN THE EARLY MORNING LIGHT, we headed for Nazareth, which Jesus called home. Along the road he told us of his early life as a carpenter and tried to teach us by way of parables, which are short stories with a deeper, more profound meaning. Unfortunately, Jesus had to keep explaining them to us, otherwise he might as well have been talking to the deaf, but he was patient and never made us feel embarrassed for asking.

We had traveled quite a distance and the crowd that was following Jesus was beginning to tire, so he stopped along the shore and got into a boat. As it drifted out, the crowd settled on the sloping bank and Jesus began to teach.

"There was a sower who went out to sow some seed. As he spread the seed, some fell on the path where the birds quickly ate them up. Some fell on rocky ground and sprouted immediately, but when the sun rose, the plants were scorched and quickly withered for lack of roots. Some fell among the thorns, and the thorns grew up and choked them. But some seed fell on good soil, and produced fruit, some thirty fold, some sixty, and some one hundred fold."

When he had finished, Matthew and Philip asked

Jesus why he spoke in parables, because as we looked at the faces in the crowd, it was obvious they had no idea what the message was supposed to be. Calling the twelve of us together he said, "To you have been given the mysteries of the kingdom of heaven, but to these it has not been granted. Therefore I speak in parables, a language they can understand."

I said, "Yes, Lord, it is in a language they understand, but what about the meaning?"

He then began to explain the parable.

"The seed is the word of God, and the seed sown on the path is the one who hears the word without understanding it, and the evil one comes and steals it away from his heart. The seed sown on the rocky ground is the one who hears the word and receives it with joy. But since he has no root, as trials or persecutions come because of the word, he falls away. The seed sown among the thorns is the one who hears the word, but then worldly anxiety and the lure of riches choke the word, and it bears no fruit. But the seed that falls on good soil is the one who hears the word and understands it, who indeed bears fruit thirty, sixty or one hundred fold."

He told one parable after another, each one tied to the kingdom of heaven. The last one he told was about good seed and weeds.

He said, "A good man sowed good seed in his field, but during the night as he slept, his enemy came and sowed weeds all through the wheat, and went away. When the wheat grew up and bore fruit, the weeds grew as well. The slaves of the householder came to him and asked, 'Sir, did we not sow good seed? Where did the weeds come from?'"

"'An enemy has done this,' he answered.

"Then the workers asked, 'Do you want us to pull up the weeds?'

"'No, if you pull up the weeds you might uproot the wheat as well. Let them grow together until harvest. At that time I will tell the harvesters to gather first the weeds and tie them in bundles for burning, but gather the wheat into my barns.'"

It was late in the evening, so Jesus dismissed the crowd. One man in the crowd, who was from that town, invited us to stay the night. So we went to his house and went in.

Once inside, I was relieved to find out that all of us needed an explanation of the last parable. Jesus was only too happy to explain that the sower was the son of God, the field was the world, and the good seed represented the children of the kingdom. The weeds were the children of the evil one and the enemy was the devil. The harvest, the end of the age, and the harvesters were the angels. It was clear then that the weeds were the sinners and the stalks of wheat were the righteous.

Finally, I understood. And I watched as eyes lit up around the room when the other listeners also grasped the meaning.

The thing that scared me the most was coming face to face with evil. Although I had heard about the devil, demons and the evil one my whole life, since I had been with Jesus not only did he talk about the devil, I saw him drive demons out of people right before my eyes. The demons would call him Son of God and come out with screams and shrieks.

He once drove demons out of two men, and they

went into a herd of swine. Immediately the pigs raced down the cliff into the lake and drowned.

It appeared we had all chosen the right side to be on. Correction, we had been chosen to be on the right side.

I remember, as a young man facing down a large dog that had gone mad. It was frightening. However, it paled in comparison to being in the vicinity of demons, especially as they were being cast out.

I was beginning to believe, without reservation that Jesus was the Christ, the son of the living God. As much as I believed this, I wondered constantly why the Son of God needed or even wanted an old sinner like myself tagging along. Surely there were many men who were more qualified to be an apostle than this simple fisherman. I guess the best thing I can do is let Jesus figure out what to do with me. After all, he's answered every riddle so far.

CHAPTER 7

ONE OF THE THINGS THAT kept me awake at night and on edge every day was the hostile surveillance by our religious leaders, as if we were criminals or rebels. The ever-watchful Pharisees and priests never missed an opportunity to try to trap Jesus with clever and well-thought-out questions. Instead of believing what they were witnessing daily with their own eyes, they continued to scheme and plot in an effort to expose Jesus as a fraud, or worse, an enemy of the Jewish Law.

For example, as Jesus sat in the temple yard teaching about the kingdom of heaven, some Pharisees and members of Herod's party approached him and said, "We admire you as a teacher, always telling the truth and not worrying about people's status or what they think." Then they asked, "Tell us, teacher, is it against Jewish Law to pay taxes to the Roman Emperor? Should we pay them or not?"

Jesus, not fooled by their false flattery, called them hypocrites and asked, "Why are you trying to trick me?" He then requested them to bring him a silver coin.

Now, I did not understand what the trick was, but I knew if Jesus said there was a trick, they had something up their sleeves. Taking the coin he asked, "Whose face and inscription is on the coin?"

"Why, it is the likeness of the Emperor," they answered with arrogance.

"Well then, render onto Caesar what is Caesar's and render onto God what is God's."

The men looked as if they had seen a ghost. I am quite sure they had prepared that question with the utmost confidence, knowing beyond any doubt, they would trap Jesus into saying something they could take back to their high priests in the Sanhedrin, but once again they left empty-handed. Defeated, yes, but with angry glares that ensured they would be back again and again if necessary, until they fulfilled their mission.

When the crowds had departed for the evening, I caught Jesus as he was going off on his own to pray, which he did every morning and evening.

"Please, explain to me how they tried to trap you today," I asked.

With the look of a loving father, eager to explain something important to his son, he said, "Had I said yes, you should pay taxes to Caesar, the Pharisees would have accused me of breaking the Jewish law. If I had said no, do not pay taxes to the emperor, they would have turned me over to Herod's men for sedition against Rome."

"My Lord," I asked. "Will I ever possess the knowledge to answer such sly questions?"

"In time, you and the others will work greater miracles than I," Jesus replied.

Calling the others around him, he questioned us, asking, "Who do people say that I am?"

"Why some say you are a prophet; others say Elijah; and still others say you are John the Baptist," they answered.

He then asked us, "And who do you say that I am?"

Before I could gather my thoughts and make a clear determination of how I was going to answer, I blurted out something—where it came from, I couldn't say. "Why, you are the Messiah, the Son of the living God," I said with the authority of an emperor.

The other disciples looked and nodded their heads in agreement, except the one named Judas. He had a peculiar expression, as if he either wasn't sure or was afraid to accept my testimony. But, after all this time with Jesus, accept it or not, no one could convince me otherwise!

"Good for you, Simon, son of John!" exclaimed Jesus. "For this truth did not come to you from a human being, but from my Father in heaven. And so Peter, I call you Cephas, and on this rock I will build my church, and the gates of hell will not prevail against it.

"I will give to you the keys to the kingdom of heaven; what you loose on earth shall be loosed in heaven, and what you bind on earth shall be bound in heaven." He then ordered us not to tell anyone he was the Messiah and he left us to pray.

How could Jesus expect me to be the foundation of his church? I couldn't recite three scriptures or answer any of the questions these hypocritical church leaders were throwing at him. I wondered how the other men felt about what they had just heard, so I asked my brother Andrew.

"Please, tell me why you think Jesus has put me in such a position, surely there are many men in these crowds and among the twelve who are much more qualified than I."

"Brother, I can't tell you which others might be qualified, but I will tell you, if the Son of the living God has deemed you the rock on which he will build his church, then from this day forward you are no longer Simon Peter but my brother, Cephas."

CHAPTER 8

THE NEXT MORNING WE LEFT early and arrived in Nazareth by noon. This crowd was different from others we had encountered. My guess is that, since most of them knew Jesus and his mother and father, it was beyond their grasp to accept that he was anything but a gifted teacher. As Jesus spoke in the synagogue, they were all amazed.

"Where did he get such wisdom and the power to perform miracles," they wondered. I don't want to call them malicious, but there was a steady murmur going through the crowd that I couldn't help but hear, so I know Jesus heard it.

"Is not this man the carpenter, son of Mary and Joseph? Surely, he is not the Messiah," they scoffed. So, the majority rejected Jesus and his teaching. This was a first. Crowds in other cities had treated him like a king, but those in his own town refused to believe.

Except for a couple of small healings, Jesus was unable to work any miracles. Jesus told them, "A prophet is accepted everywhere but in his own town and by his own family."

So we moved on.

I looked back, bewildered and almost heartbroken, knowing what these people had turned away.

"Why couldn't you do any miracles," John asked cautiously. It was the question we all wanted to ask; only the rest of us lacked the courage. Maybe there was an underlying fear that Jesus was losing his power and nobody wanted to deal with it. What in the world was I thinking? The Son of God doesn't lose his power.

Whatever took place back in Nazareth surely could be explained, and that is exactly what our Lord did.

"How could I possibly work any miracles," he answered. "They were faithless, and without faith I can do nothing."

For the first time since I had met Jesus, I saw a definite look of sorrow on his face. As he peered back over his shoulder, taking one last look at Nazareth, I couldn't help but wonder how it felt to be the Son of God and helpless at the same time.

CHAPTER 9

A S WE WERE HEADED BACK to Galilee, I looked forward to seeing familiar faces, along with the countryside that had been home for most of my life. The past year-and-a-half following Jesus had wrought changes in all of us, but for me, it was as if I had shed my skin and become a different man. I no longer walked with fear of where the journey would lead me; instead, my attention was focused on becoming as much like Jesus as humanly possible.

Jesus constantly reminded us that the lessons he taught us were not only for this world, but also for the world to come. I know the world to come is in the future, but when? I wanted to know where the Messiah would set up his kingdom here on earth, and, when he did, would we apostles have positions of authority?

Being the rock upon which Jesus would build his church didn't exactly sound like a powerful position in a kingdom. In addition to my unvoiced thoughts, some of the twelve were arguing among themselves about their future positions. Maybe Jesus had something else in mind, perhaps a new church, apart from the Pharisees and high priests, with the doctrine he teaches, but more importantly, the doctrine he lives out every day.

Judging by the crowds, whatever direction he decides to go, the people would support him all the way to the top. This isn't the case for the leaders of the church, though. Jesus makes them uneasy. Despite the fact that he never serves up a frown or turns away a person in need, that he heals people of every kind of ailment and that he even raises the dead, there isn't another man in Judea more annoying to the Pharisees than Jesus.

Some time ago, while in the temple teaching, Jesus was presented with a man whose hand was withered and paralyzed.

"Teacher, is it against the law to heal on the Sabbath?" they asked.

I absolutely loved the look Jesus exchanged with these crafty snakes. It was a look that asked, "Is that the best you can do," mixed with "Please, open your ears and hear."

With the brilliance of a scholar, Jesus answered, "What if one of you had a sheep and it fell into a deep hole on the Sabbath? Would you not take hold of it and lift it out? Is not a human worth many times more than a sheep? So then, what does our Law allow us to do on the Sabbath? To help or to harm? To save someone's life or to destroy it?"

Jesus then told the man, "Stretch out your hand."

The man's face lit up with surprise, then joy as he stretched out his hand, now made whole. Immediately the Pharisees who had brought the man to the temple turned and headed for the door. Filled with embarrassment and rage, they began discussing what they could do about Jesus, even before they were out of our hearing.

Does not what he said make good sense? I thought to myself. How can healing someone on any day be bad? But the Pharisees were a testy bunch, and the lines were being drawn in the sand.

CHAPTER 10

WHEN WE ARRIVED AT THE edge of the city, Jesus called the twelve of us together. Dividing us into pairs, he sent us forth to different regions, giving us the authority to drive out demons, heal diseases and even raise the dead. He instructed us not to carry a beggar's bag, bread or money in our pockets. Take a walking stick and your sandals, he instructed, but do not even take an extra cloak.

He also strictly told us, "Do not go into any Gentile territories or Samaritan towns. Instead, go to the lost sheep of Israel. Go and preach that the Kingdom of heaven is near! Heal the sick, raise the dead, heal those who suffer from dreaded diseases, and drive out demons. You have received without paying, so give without being paid.

"Wherever you are welcomed, stay in that same house until you leave that place. When you go into a house, say, 'Peace be with you.' If the people of that house welcome you, let your greeting of peace remain, but if they do not welcome you, take back your greeting. If some town or home will not welcome you or refuses to listen to your teaching, leave that place and shake the dust from your feet. I assure you that on Judgment Day, God will show more mercy to the people of Sodom and Gomorrah than to the people of that town."

I had been looking forward to seeing home, but now Andrew and I headed off to see if Jesus had made the right choice. It had been ages since my brother and I had time to talk freely, without the constant interruption of the crowds. I longed to get his take on all that had happened in our lives and see how he envisioned the outcome of this new movement Jesus had created.

Andrew had always been very practical, with the ability to adapt and flow with whatever life threw at him. I hoped that he was thinking about asking me the same questions.

Instead, he asked, "Can you imagine the two of us healing people and giving sight to the blind, or bringing the dead back to life! I don't know about you, brother, but that seems about as far-fetched as any dream I have ever had. I mean, it's one thing for Jesus, the Son of God, to do these things, but for you and me? I just don't know."

"Andrew, you heard the Master give us the power," I replied. "You were listening, weren't you?"

"Yes, I heard him, but I implore you to tell me, do you believe that we can do the miraculous things we have witnessed?"

Until then, no one had questioned my beliefs, so my brother's question stirred the doubt within me. I wasn't sure how my answer would come out, but I knew doubt had to go, especially if we were to have any chance of spreading the good news.

"Things have happened so fast, Andrew, I haven't had time to decide what I am sure about and what I have reservations about. I will tell you this, if Jesus said we are given the power to do these things, then why wouldn't every one of us believe? Surely, none of us can give a reason to question anything that comes from his mouth. To the contrary, we have yet to see him fail at anything or be unable to answer the doubters. So, my answer to your question is yes, *yes,* I do believe."

———————⟨✦⟩———————

It was mid-afternoon, and in the distance I could make out a small town, not much bigger than a village. There was a light breeze in our faces and, even at that distance, the aroma of fresh bread guided us toward our target.

The area was worse than most for traveling. With the rocky terrain torturing our feet and thorns tearing at our tunics, we pressed on.

"It won't be long now, brother, destiny awaits us," I said, pointing to the town.

"Yes, destiny," he nodded. "I can't help but wonder if the people in this town have ever heard of Jesus and his Kingdom."

"It's hard to say. We are more than two days' walk from Galilee, and I don't recall visiting this town. However, the way the news of Jesus has spread throughout Judea, I wouldn't be surprised in the least if we find a welcoming party on the lookout for him. But should we find the opposite, which is exactly why we are here, then we teach and heal just as Jesus told us."

Upon entering the town, I noticed a small group of men sitting around a large crackling fire, discussing the problems that a lack of rain was causing with their crops and with the grazing of their animals. We were greeted courteously and asked what brought us to this out-of-the-way town.

"We are here to tell you about the Kingdom of heaven, and the miraculous deeds done by Jesus of Nazareth," Andrew blurted out, before I could even draw a breath.

"I have heard about this man you call Jesus," said an elderly man. "My brother was in the town of Capernaum some time back where he claims he witnessed this Jesus heal a paralyzed man. He said the healing was truly amazing, but that something else really shook up the crowd. Before he healed him, this prophet forgave the man of his sins. This angered not only the Pharisees but a great many of the onlookers, causing a lot of talk about blasphemy. So, is this the same man you two are referring to? And what light can you shed on the story I was told?"

"It is, in fact the same man, and your story is correct," I replied boldly. "But that is only one of hundreds of miraculous events we have witnessed."

As we began recalling one story after another, each more impressive than the last, the men fell into a trance, hanging on every word.

It wasn't long before a young man pulled a small loaf of bread from his bag and offered it to us, saying, "I can't believe you have journeyed such a long distance without food. Surely you are famished."

I can't remember a scrap of bread tasting so good. We quickly thanked the man.

Since we had begun speaking, more than twenty

more men had gathered to hear what we had to say. One of the elders, a man who clearly demanded respect, spoke up. "Obviously this Jesus is a very special prophet, doing things that are unheard of, but where does he get his power from? Has he shared this information with you or do you just accept him at face value?"

How could I not accept him at face value after what we had witnessed for nearly two years?

"What more must a man do to garner our respect and belief," Andrew asked. "Never has there been such a prophet, whose wisdom is unmatched, teaching and healing, showing us the way to the Kingdom of heaven."

"Indeed, we are all in search of heaven, but a little heaven here on earth would be nice!" exclaimed another of the elders.

The fire was beginning to die out, and I was exhausted. I was beginning to wonder where Andrew and I would sleep when the prominent elder in the group asked, "Where do you two intend to spend the night?"

"We haven't procured a place yet," I said. "I guess we got too busy spreading the Good News and forgot about the necessities. We have spent so many nights under the stars that finding lodging never came to mind."

"I would be most honored to have you stay at my house this night, where you can share a meal and rest. I would like to hear more about this man you call Jesus," the man said.

"I think I speak for both of us when I accept your invitation, sir," I replied.

Upon arriving at the man's house, we entered and I said, "Peace be with you and on your house."

The man thanked me and accepted my offering of peace.

The following morning, a small crowd began to gather, and a blind man was among the group. Speaking in our direction, he said, "They tell me you have been sent by the prophet whose name is spreading throughout Judea on account of the miraculous deeds he has been performing."

Andrew responded, "Yes, that is true, we have been sent by Jesus to spread the good news and heal the lost sheep of Israel."

Eagerly, the man asked, "Can you heal me?"

"What is it that you would have me do for you, sir?" I asked

"I want to see! I have spent my whole life in darkness, wishing only for a glimpse of what they call the sunset," the poor man pleaded with tears streaming down his dusty cheeks.

I placed my hands on the man's eyes and said, "Be open, receive your sight!"

When I removed my hands, instead of the jubilation I had been accustomed to, the man shrieked, "I am still blind!"

Quickly Andrew repeated what I had just done, only to find the man still in darkness.

My mind was racing. What could have gone wrong and what must that crowd of angry people be contemplating for Andrew and me? I had a sick feeling in the pit of my stomach that was nearly taking me to the ground.

By now the blind man was in anguish; one minute

he was expecting to see for the first time, the next, crushed and broken by the failure of two men the crowd was now deriding as "Impostors!"

"I tell you, we were given the power to heal by Jesus, the Son of God," Andrew spoke up, with a tremor in his voice. How quickly our earlier conversation and Andrew's questions about whether we could perform such miraculous deeds jumped back into my head. I stood there not only humiliated, but lost and confused because we didn't restore sight to this blind man. I wondered why Jesus would hang us out to dry. He wouldn't; there had to be an answer, but what was it?

Like a flash of lightning going off in my head, I recalled the time in Nazareth when Jesus had the same problem. Apparently the blind man had lacked the faith required to make the healing possible. Yes, the man wanted to see, but it was more of a "Sure do hope this works" kind of faith, rather than a deep conviction that he would regain his sight. Jesus said, "Without faith, I can do nothing!"

As I was sorting this out, another man cried out, "Brother, I know you can heal me of these terrible sores if you want, please heal me!"

Without hesitating, I walked over to where the man was standing alone, placed my hands on him and said, "Your faith has healed you."

Immediately his skin was made whole, and he fell to his knees, praising God.

As the healings began to flow, the word spread and soon everyone from the village was present. When we had done all we could and felt that we had shared everything Jesus had taught us, we thanked the people of the town, gave them another blessing of peace and headed into the rising sun.

Although our time there was uplifting, I left with a heavy heart, knowing the terrible disappointment that the blind man had suffered when he opened his lifeless eyes only to find the same darkness that had surrounded him his whole life.

Somewhere in the reality of that situation, I saw how it mirrored a man closing his eyes in the darkness of death, only to find upon opening them in the afterlife that he was still in the darkness, the price of his lack of faith. You can only feel pity for such men and hope they find the faith and joy needed to lead them into the Kingdom of heaven before they leave this world.

The village was still within sight, and already the anticipation of the next city or town had both of us walking on air, completely convinced the Kingdom was starting right now.

Our travels took us through many towns in a short period of time. Everywhere we preached, people seemed to accept and embrace what we were teaching; however I wondered, was it because of the message they heard or did it all depend on the miracles? The same applied to the crowds that followed Jesus. How many would actually cling to his every word and acknowledge him as the Messiah were it not for the healing miracles? I remembered how quickly the gathering of men had turned on Andrew and me that first morning when we failed to cure the blind man. Followers are a fickle bunch. When push comes to shove, I am not sure if Jesus can really count on them.

CHAPTER 11

W E ARRIVED BACK IN GALILEE at the same time as the others. Jesus met us, saying, "I have spent much quiet time praying for you, and I long to hear about your travels and how you were received."

The excitement in each man's voice told the story. Despite a few disappointments in towns that did not welcome us or where miracles could not be worked, it appeared that his word and the good news had been spread to many out-of-the-way places, just as Jesus had hoped. The question was, did the seed fall on rocky ground or good soil?

Just the sight of Jesus and his disciples created a frenzy, and the crowds began to amass.

"I know you all are exhausted and hungry; let us withdraw to a secluded place where we can eat and rest," Jesus said. We quickly boarded a couple of boats and headed across the lake for some quiet time.

How good it was to be back in the company of Jesus. The trip had sapped my energy, and being back with him really charged me up.

Apparently, I was not the only one charged up. The crowds, having a pretty good idea where we were headed, circled around the lake by land and were waiting on the far shore when we arrived. This was perhaps the largest number of people I had seen gathered for any reason, and they had walked at a fast pace for a considerable distance to be here before us. There were at least five thousand men, plus women and children.

I was irritated by the massive intrusion, but Jesus never made a seeker of his presence feel unwelcome. He calmly got off the boat, walked up the hill and perched atop a rocky crag and began teaching. Although we weren't alone, we were afforded the opportunity to recline and enjoy the breezes that were coming off the lake.

The olive trees were in bloom, and the sweet fragrance of their flowers carried on the breeze, taking the edge off the day, allowing me to reminisce about my childhood. How many times had my brother and I climbed the olive trees in a nearby orchard in an effort to escape the stifling heat, and to avoid the chores that awaited all young boys our age. As an eldest son whose father had passed away, my chores were double that of the other boys, making such times had been hard to come by, and I had cherished every one.

It was getting late in the evening, so we approached Jesus and recommended he dismiss the crowd so they could get home or to a town to buy food.

"Feed them yourselves," Jesus said.

"Did you say feed them ourselves? Why, it would take two hundred days' wages to feed such a crowd, if indeed you could find the food," Phillip replied.

"There is a small lad here with five barley loaves and a couple of fishes," one of the disciples noted.

"Bring him to me," demanded Jesus. When the young lad had brought his small basket, Jesus took the bread and fish and looking up to heaven, he blessed them and gave thanks to God. Then Jesus ordered us to feed the people.

As if out of thin air, suddenly there were baskets full of bread and fish, and we passed them around and everyone ate what they wanted. The crowds had no idea what had just taken place, I think they assumed we had brought enough food to feed them all, not knowing all this came from five loaves and two fish.

When everyone had eaten their fill, Jesus instructed us to collect the scraps so as not to waste anything. To my astonishment, the leftover food filled twelve baskets. Twelve, what did that number mean?

Exhausted, I sat down in the shade of a date tree, lost in my imagination of a kingdom where King Jesus could heal the sick of their illnesses, feed the multitudes with little or nothing and push the Pharisees back into their own society of corruption. To me, that seemed like the ideal kingdom, the cure that would heal the wounds of centuries of slavery and domination. Even better, if possible, it appeared to be just for the nation of Israel.

It was obvious how Jesus felt about our religious leaders, because he was always calling them out. On one occasion he even called them a "brood of vipers," so what could be more perfect? A new kingdom and a new church, headed up by Jesus and the twelve of us in his court.

Suddenly, John's voice brought me back to the

present. "Get up, the master has ordered us to go back across the lake."

"OK, where is he and which boat is he riding in?"

"He said he was staying behind to pray, and he will catch up with us on the other side," someone shouted.

I told them I would stay back and wait for Jesus to finish, and then return with him by land. There were several things I wanted to discuss with the master, and I jumped at the opportunity to be alone with him for a few hours. I told the others to go ahead.

But my plans didn't last long. Almost as soon as I decided to stay, Jesus showed up and told me to go back with the others, because he didn't know how long he was going to be.

We loaded up and shoved off, but with the wind blowing from the direction we were headed, the sails were of no use. We would have to use the oars.

On average it would take us two hours to row the distance to Bethsaida, but as the night grew later, the wind blew harder. The fires we could see burning in town seemed to get no closer. The waves were manageable, but the manpower was beginning to tire, giving me the feeling we were actually losing ground.

In the darkness of night, I couldn't say with any certainty exactly where we were in relation to the shore. The sound of the men groaning at the oars, mixed with the whistling of the sail lines, let me know that this journey was headed for disaster. If we were to lose our forward momentum, we would be at the mercy of the wind and waves, and in the black of night that is no place to be.

Suddenly, James yelled at the top of his voice as he pointed into the darkness, "Look, it's a ghost!"

As we peered into the darkness, sure enough, there seemed to be the image of a man walking on the water. Fear gripped the tired men at the oars, and some of them began to scream in terror.

From the image came the familiar voice of Jesus, clear and calm above the wind. "Courage, it is I. Don't be afraid."

Here we were in the middle of the Sea of Galilee, and a body that appeared to be Jesus was walking on the water, telling us not to be afraid! How could he expect us to experience anything but fear?

Although I was terrified, I felt the only way to calm the others and know for sure whether or not this was really Jesus was to ask him to order me to come out onto the water with him. So that is exactly what I did, and Jesus replied, "Come!"

Without a second thought, I exited the boat and began walking across the water toward Jesus. But as I made my way toward him, the lapping of the waves against my ankles began to weaken whatever strength my faith had given me. Slowly, my feet began to sink beneath the water, and it wasn't long before the cold waves were pounding my chest.

Try as I might, I couldn't get back on top of the water as the fear of drowning began to consume me. I went into full panic mode, thrashing and screaming for Jesus like a small child who had just gone down for the first time. Although I was not a particularly good swimmer, I rarely panicked in the water. I remember screaming, "Help me, Lord!"

All of a sudden his hand grabbed mine, and

the next thing I knew we were again walking on the water.

As we neared the boat, Jesus asked, "Why did you doubt? What little faith you have!"

We got into the boat and as the wind died down, I sat there ashamed of myself, not wanting to look anyone in the eye, especially Jesus. I felt as if I had let him down.

Faith is something a person can be sure he has, but under pressure, it can be as fleeting as the wind. I sank in the water for the same reason the blind man didn't receive his sight. At least he had an excuse; he didn't know who Jesus was.

As I sat there in my mental turmoil, I don't know if I lost track of time or if it really happened, but it suddenly seemed that we were at the shore in an instant.

We unloaded, and I found a quiet place away from all the others, hoping for some reflection and prayer to calm the turbulence inside me. I couldn't explain why someone who had spent so much time with Jesus could possibly lose faith. I made myself a promise that regardless of what might confront me, never again would my faith in Jesus wane.

CHAPTER 12

THE NEXT DAY, THE CROWDS of people gathered again. It didn't matter where or how far we went, they always seemed to find Jesus. I understood their motives, listening to Jesus never got old. He would talk for hours at a stretch, and after he was done, you couldn't tell if it had been ten minutes or ten hours. Everything was about peace, love and forgiveness.

I remember one day where speaking to a very large gathering near the lake shore, Jesus said some of the most astonishing things anyone there had ever heard. He told us to love our enemies and to pray for those who persecute us.

That went against every Jewish teaching, not to mention every human instinct. How could he expect any of us to pray for the Roman vermin that have trampled over the Jewish people? But, as usual, he followed up on his teachings with explanations: If you love only those who love you, what merit is there in that? Even the tax collectors do that. If you greet only your brothers, what is unusual about that? Even the pagans do the same. What he was telling us started to make sense, it was not any easier to digest, mind you, but certainly the lamp was lit.

He talked about adultery, oaths, revenge,

divorce, false prophets and judging others—almost everything that related to human interaction. One of my favorites, which he called "The Rule," was simple but powerful: "Do unto others as you would have them do unto you."

I don't know about everyone else who heard that, but I felt that a man could pretty much live his life by that rule.

When the Master concluded that sermon, like us, the crowdswere absolutely amazed by the wisdom and authority of his words.

One enthusiastic young man ran up to Jesus and asked, "What must I do to gain eternal life?"

Jesus answered him, "If you want to enter eternal life, keep the commandments."

The young man asked, "Which ones?"

"You shall not kill, you shall not steal, you shall not bear false witness, honor your father and your mother, and love your neighbor as yourself."

At this the young man's face lit up, "All of these things I have done my entire life. What do I still lack?"

Jesus said to him, "If you want to be perfect, go and sell all that you have and give it to the poor, and then you will have treasure in heaven. Then come and follow me."

The young man was devastated. He turned and walked away with his head down, as if he had lost all that was dear to him. We learned that he was a very wealthy man with many possessions, which gave Jesus an opportunity to make a point.

"Amen, I say to you, it will be hard for one who is rich to enter the kingdom of heaven. Again, I say, it will be easier for a camel to pass through the eye of the needle than for one who is rich to enter the kingdom of God."

That caught all of us off guard.

"If no rich man can get into the kingdom of God, who then can be saved?" we asked.

Jesus answered quickly, "For men it is impossible, but not for God. All things are possible for God."

For the first time in my life, I was hearing that a rich man doesn't have the best chance at something. Not only that, but according to Jesus, great wealth could prove to be an insurmountable obstacle to entering the kingdom.

It didn't take long before the twelve of us began to point out to Jesus how we had given up everything we owned to follow him, making us very poor indeed. The fact that Jesus already knew everything I had done did not stop me from reminding him. After all, this was the eternal kingdom that was at stake.

It wasn't only me. The rest of the group was making sure their voices were heard.

Jesus said, "Amen, I say to you that you who have followed me, in the new age when the Son of Man is seated on his throne of glory, you will yourselves sit on twelve thrones judging the twelve tribes of Israel. And everyone who has given up his house or brothers or sisters, mothers or fathers or children or lands for my sake and the sake of the gospel will receive much more in this present age. They will receive a hundred times more houses, brothers, mothers, sisters, children and fields, including persecutions as well, but they will receive eternal life in the age to come."

At last I had made the connection to the number

twelve! Since we would rule over Israel and the twelve tribes, giving up everything to follow Jesus had been an excellent choice.

Although I could see how his popularity could eventually put Jesus in a position to be a king, getting out from under Roman dominion would not be quite so easy. In addition, the high priests and Pharisees were not going to sit idly by and allow Jesus to set up his kingdom and church, leaving them on the outside looking in. No, as I have always contended, this was a ruthless bunch and they were not going away without a fight. A fight, I am afraid, in which they were willing to pull out all the stops, even going so far as to solicit help from the pagan Romans.

During this time, Jesus was simply going from town to town preaching the truth and healing the sick, yet the Pharisees already perceived him as a threat and were slinking around like a pack of jackals, trying to find a way to take him down. These men enjoyed their places of honor far too much to ever be reduced to the status of a common man, and even with the crowd's support of Jesus, there would likely be bloodshed when he came into his kingdom.

Over a period of a few weeks, I began to sense an urgency about Jesus, as if he were making last-minute preparations for a trip. We didn't stay in places quite as long as we once did, and he seemed to stay closer to Jerusalem.

During one short journey, as we were traveling between towns, Jesus told us that he must go into Jerusalem and suffer greatly at the hands of the elders, chief priests and scribes. He said that he would be *killed* and on the third day be raised up from the dead.

I could not believe what I was hearing, and it definitely left the others unsettled. Surely Jesus was speaking in parables, or were we misunderstanding his meaning, because not long ago he was telling us we would sit on thrones and judge the twelve tribes of Israel. How would this ever come to pass if he were dead?

I asked him to repeat what he had said, just to make sure we had heard him correctly.

When he again said the same things, I exclaimed, "No way, Lord! God forbid anything like that should happen!"

Then he said something to me that cut me to my core.

"Get behind me, Satan! You are an obstacle to me. You are not thinking as God does, but as human beings do."

Upon hearing this rebuke, I was too bewildered to think, let alone speak. How did he expect me to think? After all, I am a human being. One minute I was ready to make sure no harm would befall Jesus, the next I am being accused of being Satan. How could Jesus distort my motive, making me out to be such a bad guy, when I would die for him?

A while later as we rested, James and John came and sat by me. They explained their take on what our Lord had said. I listened to what they had to say, eventually accepting the fact that Jesus was probably referring to Satan working through me, not that I was actually Satan. We still did not understand why he said those things, and we made certain to discuss the matter only when Jesus was away from us praying.

The thing that gripped us with fear more than anything else was the fear of something happening to Jesus. Where would that leave us? No king could mean only one thing—no kingdom!

On the positive side, it was hard for me to imagine the crowds allowing anything to happen to Jesus. No, the only way any harm could come to him would be if the Romans felt threatened. Even then, they would have to act quickly, because if the entire nation of Israel joined together behind Jesus, Rome's hold on us would disappear.

CHAPTER 13

A S WE MADE OUR WAY toward Capernaum, we reached the foot of a mountain. Jesus told us all to sit down and rest. Then he instructed James, John and me to follow him up the slope. It was a rugged climb, and I couldn't for the life of me figure out why we were climbing to the top of what appeared to be just a rocky mountain.

"Lord, must we go all the way to the top," John asked hesitantly.

"I need to be alone with you," was the response. I did know one thing: mountain climbing is an activity best left to the young guys.

After reaching the summit, we came to a clearing. Jesus moved away a short distance from us and as he did, his clothes became a dazzling, blinding white. They were so bright it hurt my eyes to look at him. The brightness was similar to the sun shimmering off of a lake. As amazing as his clothes were, his face shone even brighter than the sun.

Shielding our eyes, the three of us looked at each other, wondering what was about to happen. Suddenly, there were two men standing with Jesus and talking to him. We believed them to be Moses and Elijah. We were all excited and I told Jesus, "How good it is that we are here. If you wish we can make three tents, one for you, one for Moses and one for Elijah ..."

Before I could finish speaking, out of nowhere came a shining cloud that settled over the three. It was one of the most incredible things I had ever witnessed, yet I had no idea what it meant. There came a loud voice from the cloud, saying, "This is my beloved son, with whom I am well pleased. Listen to him!"

The voice was like no other I had ever heard, and it terrified all of us. I fell to the ground and shielded my face, fairly certain I did not want to see who that voice was attached to.

But to my surprise, the next thing I knew, Jesus was touching me and saying, "Get up, don't be afraid." Struggling to my feet, I saw no one except him. I knew my world had dramatically changed. By now I should have been prepared for anything, but I am fairly certain something like that would have scared anyone.

We headed down the mountain with no explanation to speak of. As we descended, Jesus told us not to tell anyone what we had seen until the Son of Man had been raised from the dead.

James probed further by asking, "Why do the teachers of the law say that Elijah must come first?"

"Elijah is indeed coming first," answered Jesus. "And he will get everything ready. But I tell you that Elijah has already come and the people did not recognize him, but instead they treated him just as they pleased, in the same way they will mistreat the Son of Man."

As we lagged behind, we discussed the fact that

Jesus must have been referring to John the Baptist. I remember listening to John preaching at the river Jordan; he said he was preparing the way of the Lord. To say he was mistreated was an understatement. Being imprisoned for telling a king the truth and later being beheaded by the same cruel and ruthless king goes far beyond mistreatment. I was quite sure, however, that when Jesus was in power, those days of cruel and unjust punishment would become a thing of the past, or at least reserved for those who richly deserved it.

I felt as did the rest of the group that all the traveling we had done was Jesus' way of gaining the support he needed from all areas of Judea. When the time was right, a kingdom ruled by the Messiah would be born, and it would be made possible by the tens of thousands of followers who loved Jesus and would do anything necessary to assure his triumph.

I know Jesus said he would endure much suffering, but I couldn't imagine the crowds allowing anything to happen to their new hope. Why, I could hardly get to Jesus when the crowds were present, let alone do him any harm. I hoped, for the sake of that dream, that Jesus was wrong and his kingdom would eventually take root and be realized. That was only one man's opinion, but I really believed his kingdom and church would and could change men, not just now but forever.

As we walked along, the three of us who witnessed what had taken place on the mountaintop tried to understand what we had seen and why we were permitted to see it. I did know one thing, I had seen John the Baptist in person and that was not John up on that mountain. Whatever it meant, it was another absolutely astounding experience, one I would remember forever.

CHAPTER 14

A S WE WERE HEADED TO Jerusalem, Jesus mentioned he was hungry. Just ahead on the side of the road was a fig tree, completely covered with leaves.

Jesus went ahead of us, searching the tree for figs but found nothing. I don't think he realized it, but it wasn't the right time for figs to be on the tree; however that did not stop Jesus from cursing the tree, saying, "You will never again bear fruit!"

We all heard him, but no one questioned his reasoning.

I could always tell when we were getting close to Jerusalem by the acrid odor of burning trash. Outside the city walls was a continuously burning dump that never went out. Everything imaginable was thrown into it and burned.

We arrived in the city and made our way to the temple. Inside, I saw an endless number of money changers and merchants selling pigeons, doves and animals. It seemed more like a marketplace than a place for worshipping God, and that seemed to annoy Jesus immensely. He strode angrily to one of the money changers, grabbed his table and sent it end over end into the wall, spilling everything that was on it. His anger grew into a full rage as he went from table to table, scattering birds, animals and money all over the outer temple floor.

Then he fashioned a whip from a length of rope and while he never actually hit anyone with it, he sent animals and men scurrying for the safety of the courtyard as he shouted at the top of his voice, "My temple should be a house of prayer, but you have made it a den of thieves! Get out!"

I tell you, I was so dumbfounded you could have knocked me over with a feather. In all the years I had spent with him, Jesus had never shown that kind of hostility or any kind of aggression. And if we were caught off guard, you should have seen the expression on the faces of the chief priests and teachers of the Law.

Jesus had an immense number of followers, and the temple and its courtyard were filled with as many of them as could crowd inside. To a man, they clearly agreed with that temple outburst. I believed the whole scene frightened the very life out of every scribe, teacher of the Law and priest that was present, sending them out into the streets to gather before scurrying off to their secret meeting places.

Jesus apologized to no one, but looked sternly satisfied as if he had tended to a matter that had needed his attention for a long time.

We left the city, heading for the quiet of the hillsides to spend the night. Walking the same road we traveled coming in, I noticed the very fig tree that Jesus had cursed was dead down to its roots. Amazed, I said, "Look, teacher, the tree you cursed has died!"

Jesus answered, "I assure you that if you believe

and do not doubt, you will be able to do what I have done to this fig tree. Not only this, but you will be able to say to this mountain, 'Get up and throw yourself into the sea,' and it will. If you believe, you will receive whatever you ask for in prayer."

Later that night as we talked among ourselves, I pointed out how doing the right thing had no bounds, no matter who it upset. Our Master had proved this time and time again, and I wanted to make sure the twelve of us were clear about the position we were to take while under fire.

I said twelve, but looking around I noticed Judas was missing. This struck me as odd, one of us out alone, especially considering what had taken place in the temple today.

Of all the apostles, if someone was missing it was usually Judas. I couldn't put my finger on it, but there was something about that man that never sat right with me. I don't mean to imply that any of us were exceptionally brave mind you, but Judas seemed to be a coward, never wanting to ruffle the feathers of anyone, especially the temple crowd.

One thing I learned from Jesus is that right is right, no matter whom you have to offend to make your point. But whenever a decision was on the line I observed that Judas would rather ride the tide of least resistance, making him a very weak link indeed.

The way the waters were beginning to get muddy, the last thing we needed among us was someone trying to hedge his bets by straddling the fence. There was no way to follow Jesus and his teachings without getting under the skin of most of the religious leaders, and I simply didn't believe Judas had the heart for what Jesus was asking.

That's not to say there weren't a few men in the temple group who admired Jesus. Some of them saw Jesus as a great prophet and listened respectfully to his teachings, but none of them dared to express their belief that Jesus was the Messiah, the son of the living God, prophesied about for centuries.

I will say this, as far as Jesus was concerned either you believed or you didn't. He wasn't going to beg you. You either used the light of his teaching to light your path to life, or went away to face your demons in the darkness of sin. As compassionate as Jesus was, he refused to force anyone to believe in what he was teaching or in himself.

I recall a time in the town of Capernaum when he was teaching in the synagogue. I believe it was the day after Jesus fed thousands. Many from the same crowd that had been fed showed up and Jesus said to them, "You are looking for me not because of the signs but because you ate the loaves and were filled. Do not work for food that will perish but for the food that endures for eternal life, which the Son of Man will give you. For on him the Father, God, has set his seal."

Then they asked him, "What can we do to accomplish the works of God?"

Jesus answered, "This is the work of God, that you believe in the one he sent."

They immediately asked him what sign he could perform so they might see and believe in him.

Where were all these fools the day before? Surely they didn't really think we had carried enough provisions in the boats to feed over five thousand people. But there they stood, asking our Lord for a sign. They proclaimed, "Our ancestors ate manna in the desert, as it is written: 'He gave them bread from heaven to eat.' "

So Jesus said to them, "Amen, amen, I say to you, it was not Moses who gave the bread from heaven; my Father gives you the true bread from heaven. For the bread of God is that which comes down from heaven and gives life to the world."

In response they shouted, "Sir, give us this bread always."

Jesus said to them, "I am the bread of life. Whoever comes to me will never hunger, and whoever believes in me will never thirst. But I have told you that although you have seen me, you do not believe. Everything that the Father gives to me will come to me, and I will not reject anyone who comes to me, because I have come down from heaven not to do my own will but the will of the one who sent me. And this is the will of the one who sent me: that I should not lose anything of what he gave me, but that I should raise it on the last day. For this is the will of my Father: that everyone who sees the Son and believes in him may have eternal life, and I shall raise him on the last day."

When Jesus had finished saying that, all of the Jews in the crowd began whispering among themselves, and it was easy to hear what they were saying. They were repeating what Jesus had said about being the bread that came down from heaven and asking: How could this man have come down from heaven? Is not Joseph this man's father? Do we not know his family?

I couldn't explain it. Many of these people had known Jesus since his birth, yet he stood in their presence and said he had come down from heaven. I'd known Jesus only a couple of years, but what I had seen certainly did nothing to dismiss his claim of having come down from heaven. Maybe he was speaking in some sort of parable and the people just didn't understand it. If he was, I did not understand it either.

However, once again there was no backing off what he had said, just the message of truth straight from his heart. Jesus answered them saying, "Stop murmuring among yourselves. No one can come to me unless the Father who sent me summons him, and I will raise him on the last day. It is written in the prophets: 'They shall all be taught by God.' Everyone who listens to my Father and learns from him comes to me. Not that anyone has seen the Father except the one who is from God; he has seen the father. Amen, Amen, I say to you, whoever believes has eternal life. I am the bread of life. Your ancestors ate the manna in the desert, but they died; this is the bread that comes down from heaven so one may eat it and not die. I am the living bread that came down from heaven; whoever eats this bread will live forever; and the bread that I will give is my flesh for the life of the world."

As soon as these words reached the crowd, it was if they had been doused in fuel and set ablaze. There was anger and fighting, as people acted as if they had gone mad. I had never seen a group this large lose control that quickly. Many headed toward home, muttering to themselves and their companions about what they had just heard. Most were asking the question, "How can this man give us his flesh to eat?"

Surely Jesus had a special meaning for what he had just told this multitude, but what it was I could not say. With his usual calm demeanor and self-confidence he answered them, but I will tell you, it definitely was not what they wanted to hear, nor was it what I expected.

"Amen, amen, I say to you," Jesus continued. "Unless you eat the flesh of the Son of Man and drink his blood, you do not have life within you. Whoever eats my flesh and drinks my blood has eternal life, and I will raise him on the last day. For my flesh is true food and my blood is true drink. Whoever eats my flesh and drinks my blood remains in me and me in him. Just as the living Father sent me, and I have life because of the Father, so also the one who feeds on me will have life because of me. This is the bread that came down from heaven. Unlike your ancestors who ate and still died, whoever eats this bread will live forever."

I thought to myself, did I hear that right? Did Jesus, in fact, just tell everyone here that he was going to give them his flesh to eat and his blood to drink? I stood there shocked and in disbelief, wondering, yet almost knowing what these words would do for his popularity, not only with the crowds, but also with the leaders of the temple.

Why would a man, whether he is the Messiah or just a prophet from God, say something so unbelievable and off the charts that the kingdom he had been building would be shaken right off its foundations? My heart ached to stop time and ask Jesus what he meant by those disturbing words. I knew he wasn't crazy or a madman, as the crowd seemed to be concluding, but I really could find no fault in what they were thinking, as I was at a loss for an explanation myself.

All I could think was that Jesus would take time to explain to these people what he really meant and bring the crowd back to their senses. Was I ever wrong. Not only was the crowd, but many of his disciples were now saying, "This teaching is hard; who can accept it?"

Jesus looked around at his closest disciples, as if to let them know he knew what they were whispering. Then, without another word of explanation he asked them, "Does this shock you? What if you were to see the Son of Man ascending to where he was before? It is the spirit that gives life, while the flesh is of no avail. The words I have spoken to you are spirit and life. But there are some of you here who do not believe."

CHAPTER 15

ONE TIME WHILE WE WERE talking with Jesus, he seemed to let on that he knew who believed and who would follow him. I don't know how he knew these things, but I was certainly glad I didn't possess that unique talent. Can you imagine looking into a crowd of people and already knowing who is your enemy or friend and which ones will never believe what you are teaching?

Although Jesus was in the constant company of many people, I always got the feeling his world was self-inclusive. We were unable to penetrate beyond where he set the limits, yet he poured himself out on a daily basis, never hiding behind his words or refusing to explain their meaning. Jesus, for a lack of a better word, was a true enigma. When you listened to him, on the one hand he seemed as shallow as a puddle, but at the same time his knowledge and wisdom was as deep as the sea. Never had I seen a man with all the qualities Jesus possessed, and to top it off, he loved everyone he met.

While I truly believe that all of his close followers, the twelve if you will, looked at Jesus in a different light than the rest of the disciples and crowd, there was still room for improvement in our faith.

Jesus concluded, saying, "For this reason I have

told you that no one can come to me unless it is granted him by my Father."

Many of the people never heard his last words because they were still grumbling and gathering their belongings, preparing for their journey back to wherever they came from.

I was deeply saddened by that exodus, knowing from past experience that whatever Jesus was trying to say to them was simply being misunderstood. As Jesus stood, watching countless misguided folks leaving in such haste that a dust cloud was beginning to rise, I wondered when he would stop them. Overcome by the anxiety of the moment, I shouted, "Wait! Let us give this man an opportunity to clarify what he has just said."

But to my surprise, Jesus turned to us and asked, "Do you also want to leave?"

This was the biggest crossroad I had come to since leaving my boat and saying yes to Jesus.

We glanced back and forth at each other, our eyes begging for someone to take the reins and answer him. My brother Andrew fixed his eyes on me and nodded in the direction of Jesus, and I knew I had been selected to speak up.

"Master, to whom shall we go? You have the words of eternal life. We have come to believe and are convinced that you are the Holy One of God."

I could see a calming peace come over his face, perhaps relief to know that everyone wasn't going to leave. Yet, he exuded a confidence as if to say, I already knew. This particular teaching was not only hard for those present that day, but as the news of what Jesus had said reached the towns, the Pharisees' case against Jesus raged.

Jesus looked at us and I could tell something was tugging at his heart. He didn't keep us in the dark very long. His calmness was in sharp contrast to his stunning words: "Did I not choose you twelve? Yet one of you is a devil."

I remembered the last time he referred to one of us as a devil, it was me he was referring to. Surely, Jesus wasn't talking about me this time around, but who was it?

If I had to pick one of the twelve who was on shaky ground, it would have to be Judas. I had been convinced since he joined us that there was a dark side to him. I couldn't say for certain that Judas was the one Jesus was referring to, but he definitely was my pick.

Many nights, as the fire surrendered its light and stars took its place, we shared our thoughts, traded dreams and mostly wondered where this path would lead us. However, I recall that on many occasions, Judas was not there with us. One night in particular when I asked if anyone knew of his whereabouts, Phillip answered, "I think he is out trying to gather financial support. You do know we need some kind of help if this mission is to succeed."

I was unable to hold my tongue. "Phillip, for two-and-a-half years we have traveled nearly every foot of Judea and the surrounding countryside, and I have yet to see us rely on anything Judas has produced. I'm not saying what he contributes isn't important; it is but what I'm saying is that what Jesus says and how we talk amongst ourselves is going to be the difference between defeat and victory when the powers that be bring the heat on to try to destroy

Jesus and us. You mark my words, these things will come to pass, and it will be how we stick together that makes the difference."

I just felt that Judas was along for the ride, thoroughly enjoying the attention but not really buying into everything Jesus taught. He certainly wanted to distance himself from us when Jesus said something that went against the grain. Since Jesus did that a lot, Judas stayed on the fringe of our inner circle. I really hoped that none of us were devils and that I was wrong, but I knew one thing was sure: Jesus was always right, and when my gut feeling was that strong, so was I.

CHAPTER 16

A T THAT TIME THERE WAS a large feast going on but Jesus chose not to make his presence known, on account of the Pharisees and chief priests who were out to arrest him. It was the same old story; they refused to believe that Jesus was a prophet, let alone the Messiah. His teachings angered them, mostly because they knew he had never studied scripture, yet not one of them could hold a candlestick to Jesus when it came to scripture.

When it came to this group it was never about reason, but rather about pride which was the motivating factor that fueled their hatred for Jesus. The people were still mostly in favor of Jesus, but now the crowds were sprinkled with naysayers and doubters. For the life of me, I didn't know what else Jesus could do to keep those people on our side of the fence. How could questions about a man's place of origin blind so many people to the tremendous miracles and signs he performed; not behind closed doors mind you, but right out in the open, in broad daylight for all to witness.

What I used to believe was a sure thing, the people backing Jesus and his kingdom, was now far from certain. The crowds changed from minute to minute, never standing on their own two feet but letting the wind of persuasion blow them where it willed. And now we are told that someone in our inner circle is not willing to stand with Jesus and the rest of us. There was one thing I knew for certain, I'd never desert him, even if it cost me my life.

All that being said, Jesus quietly made his way to the feast of the Tabernacles, and from there he went straight to the temple area to teach. As he taught, he asked them, "Why are you trying to kill me?" They answered him by asking if he was possessed, and who it was that was trying to kill him. It was strange; although many of the officials wanted to arrest him, no one dared to make a move. Even the temple guards sent by the high priests left without their prey.

The tension eventually eased and everyone went to their homes that evening, but Jesus went to the Mount of Olives to pray. With the light of day came the light of the world, a title Jesus had given himself some time earlier. And truly, if you listened to what Jesus had to say, his ideals and teachings would make the world a brighter place. How could love, repentance for one's sins and forgiveness produce anything else ... that is, as long as everyone subscribed to his way of living?

Jesus always approached his teaching the same way, straightforward and to the point, a point which never wavered or was affected by the disagreement of others. He took up his place in the temple area that he had surrendered the evening before, picking up right where he left off.

Although the substance of what he said never changed, I could see a difference in Jesus. There was a tiredness in his eyes that reached out to a person's soul, begging to be heard and more importantly, to be understood. At times I wanted to put my arm around him and thank him for giving me the opportunity to share his life, but I never did. He seemed to feel my adoration and gratitude without me ever having to tell him.

Jesus had not been teaching long when the scribes and Pharisees dragged a woman into the courtyard, casting her to the ground in front of Jesus and the entire crowd. That ruthless bunch had no intention of leaving Jesus to his teaching. They were going to find a way to arrest him and turn the crowd against him, no matter who they trampled in the process.

They stood her up in front of the entire crowd, saying, "Teacher, this woman was caught in the very act of committing adultery. Now, in the law, Moses commanded us to stone such a woman. So what do you say?"

It had to be humiliating for the woman to not only be caught in this position, but being dragged in front of all these people, some of whom you might have committed this same act with, must have been devastating.

It was easy to know what line of work she was in by her lavish clothing and the strong fragrance of her perfume. There was nothing subtle about it. It was a perfume preferred by prostitutes because of its ability to overpower and mask other smells.

I felt sorry for her. Naturally I recognized the sin, but after all this time with Jesus I was beginning to understand compassion.

Jesus gave this self-righteous mob only the slightest glance. Bending down, he began to write with his finger in the sand. I leaned in closer, hoping to read what the master was writing. The curious elders in the crowd also inched forward for a peek. I was several feet from Jesus, but it looked as if he was writing names and, beside the names, a list of their sins. I couldn't believe my eyes. Who could possibly know this kind of information? Most of these people were strangers to us.

The scribes continued to badger him for an answer, until Jesus finally stood up and said, "Let the one among you who is without sin be the first to cast a stone at her." He then calmly bent down and continued writing on the ground.

The hostile crowd fell silent. No muttering. No muffled whispers. Just seconds before, the same throng had been drunk with rage in anticipation of stoning a woman to death. I felt there were many in the crowd who now would like to see that woman go away, taking with her the knowledge of their sins.

The men looked at each other in amazement, not only shocked by how Jesus had turned the tables but disturbed beyond belief by what had been scrawled in the sand. The word *hypocrisy* had never been more clearly illustrated, and unlike some of the Master's parables which sometimes were hard to understand, this lesson was as clear as crystal.

Being exposed to their own sinfulness and called out in front of their friends seemed to be too much for the elders. They were the first to drop their stones and leave with their heads hung in shame. The Pharisees, temple priests and the entire crowd left in a similar fashion, dragging their chains of iniquity.

The silence was broken by Jesus when he asked,

"Woman, where are they? Has no one condemned you?"

This frightened woman, who had just escaped certain death due to the intervention of Jesus, replied, "No one, sir."

He looked at her with the love of a father who had just finished chastising his child and said, "Neither do I condemn you. Go, and from now on do not sin anymore."

I had seen many men and women healed over the years, many leaving without a thank you, but not this woman. One could tell that this was a life-changing experience for her, and her former ways of life were over. Indeed, this turned out to be the case as she became a very loyal disciple of our Lord.

It was becoming all too clear that the Jewish people were being intimidated by the very people who were supposed to lead them to God. There was division in families, and when Jesus was the topic of discussion, even the church elders could not agree with one another. Many who wanted to believe feared the ridicule and persecution of their peers, so they chose not to make their true feelings known.

I remember Jesus saying, "I have not come to bring peace, but rather division between a man and his wife, a man against his father, and a daughter against her mother. Whoever loves his father or mother more than me is not worthy of me."

I guess that pretty much summed it up; it was Jesus first or you were wasting your time.

The controversy with the fallen woman in no way stopped our Lord from continuing his mission to teach and preach. Quite the contrary, while in

Jerusalem during the Feast of Dedication, Jesus walked about in the temple area where the Jews gathered around him. "How long do you intend to keep us in suspense," they asked him. "If you are the Messiah, tell us plainly."

"I told you and you do not believe," Jesus replied. "The works I do in my Father's name testify to me. But you do not believe because you are not among my sheep. My sheep hear my voice; I know them, and they follow me. I give them eternal life, and they shall never perish. No one can take them out of my hand. My Father, who has given them to me, is greater than all, and no one can take them out of the Father's hand. The Father and I are one."

Immediately, the elders among the group started gathering rocks to stone him.

Jesus addressed them, "I have shown you many good works from my Father. For which of these are you trying to stone me?"

They shouted back, "We are not stoning you for a good work, but for blasphemy. You, a man, are making yourself God."

Again Jesus answered them, "Is it not written in your law, 'I said, "You are gods" '? If it calls them gods to whom the word of God came, and scripture cannot be set aside, can you say that the one whom the Father has consecrated and sent into the world blasphemes because I said, "I am the Son of God?"

"If I do not perform my Father's works, do not believe me; but if I perform them, even if you do not believe me, believe the works so that you may realize and understand that the Father is in me and I am in the Father."

Once again Jesus had put the ball in their court, making them see their own inability to understand the scriptures, and that always ended with anger. They threatened to arrest him, but Jesus mixed in among the crowd and slipped away.

CHAPTER 17

WE FOUND OURSELVES ON THE banks of the river Jordan, where John the Baptist had spent a great deal of time baptizing and preaching repentance. Small groves of trees provided shade from the relentless sun, and the sound of running water was soothing to the soul.

It wasn't exactly like being back on the Sea of Galilee with the waves lapping gently against the boat and the sails fluttering effortlessly in the breeze, but it was definitely a pleasant place to unwind and gather one's thoughts. We all enjoyed the opportunity to recharge our spirits.

Even Jesus seemed a bit relieved with this temporary break from the crowds. I say temporary because that is what it usually was because the people would eventually find Jesus regardless of where he was. This time turned out to be no different. However, the crowds that gathered here at the Jordan seemed to be more in touch with what Jesus was trying to teach and appeared to believe in him.

Many of these people had heard John the Baptist. John had not performed any signs, but he had prophesied that many signs would be performed by the one who would follow him, and that one would be the Messiah. I listened to all these strangers talking about what John had said, describing the one who would come after him and it surely appeared that Jesus fit the description.

Every time Jesus seemed to be reaching the multitudes, the religious leaders tried to turn the people of Israel against him. As Jesus' popularity grew, the temple crowd became even more vocal about their desires to have him arrested or do him harm. But why? Jesus never preached anything but love and peace, all the while doing miraculous healings, the likes of which have never been seen. It didn't make sense to me. I suspected there was more to their evil ways than a man like me could ever know, but they kept that secret from the people.

Early on during our third day at the Jordan, several strangers appeared on the opposite bank, calling to us from across the river. "Master, the one you love is ill!"

"Who is it? Who is ill," we all asked at once.

Walking out into the shallows, Jesus called across to the strangers, "This illness is not to end in death, but is for the glory of God that the Son of God may be glorified through it."

One could not have asked for a better answer, I thought. It was apparent, however, that these folks were hoping Jesus would come back with them to Bethany to attend to their friend personally. We again questioned Jesus for the man's name that had brought these people such a distance in search of help.

"Lazarus, the brother of Martha and Mary," Jesus replied.

I don't recall the Master giving it another thought, but if he did, I couldn't tell. He just went about telling the crowd how they could save their souls by repentance of their sins and loving one another.

How simple, I thought, everyone can do that.

A couple of days later, I had risen earlier than the rest and was watching a shepherd water his small flock of sheep a short stretch down the river. The sound of the lambs crying out reminding their mothers not to leave them took me to a time long ago.

It was a time when my father was still alive. Andrew was just a small boy, and I was nearly ten years of age. On rare occasions my father would not take to the sea, but would instead take us into the countryside to pick figs and dates from the trees on his brother's land. We had to pass a large sheep farm, where the owner would let my brother and I hold and pet the lambs. They would cry for their mothers until we put them down, then they would scurry back into the flock, quickly locating mom for a feeding. This was as close to having a pet as I ever got. Feeding ourselves was difficult enough; a pet was a luxury we could not afford.

As I was reliving my youth, Jesus startled me with a tap on my shoulder.

"Let us go back to Judea."

"Did I hear you right? Why would we return to Judea," I asked. "Master, surely you haven't forgotten the way you were treated there just a few short days ago?"

"They wanted to stone you and probably us too," John said.

These days I rarely questioned anything Jesus

wanted to do, but this seemed like a terrible mistake, one that could bring about the deadly consequences Jesus had referred to some time earlier. And those consequences were my greatest fear.

The Master had to know the things that worried me were real indeed, yet just as he always preached the truth without fear of retaliation, off we went in search of his sick friend Lazarus.

"You know Master, we can travel by night which would reduce our chances of being arrested or the crowds giving away our position," I suggested to Jesus.

"Are there not twelve hours in a day? If one walks during the day, he does not stumble because he sees the light of this world. But if one walks at night, he stumbles because the light is not in him." After saying this, he turned and headed in the direction of Bethany. It was settled. If those evildoers were set on arresting Jesus and possibly us, we were going to make it as easy for them as possible.

I started thinking maybe I had a little coward in me, but I quickly erased that thought by telling myself that what I had suggested just made good sense. How could the message about the good news be spread if we were all in jail or even worse, dead? Someone in the group needed to be concerned with our self-preservation. Jesus certainly wasn't, and yet he was the one they wanted the most.

As we walked on, these thoughts went back and forth in my head. As I tried to convince myself that things would be all right, another part of me knew that we would eventually run out of luck.

In the midst of all that thinking I remembered

something Jesus had said: "Whoever seeks to preserve his life will lose it, but whoever loses his life for my sake will save it."

I remember how noble those words sounded in a tranquil setting. However, when faced with the possibility of this actually becoming a reality, they seemed to have lost their luster. Looking into the eyes of the other men, I could tell I was not alone with my fears, but if Jesus was willing to take the risk, then so would we.

As we walked, Jesus casually mentioned that this fellow Lazarus was only asleep and that he was going to awaken him. Now I was really upset, not only was this a very risky trip, but we were making it for a friend who was not even seriously ill, only asleep.

Several apostles said, "Master if he is asleep then he will be saved."

But this time Jesus said, "Lazarus has died. And I am glad for you that I was not there, that you may believe. Let us go to him."

Arriving in Bethany, we came across groups of friends who had come to mourn and help comfort the family. This man Lazarus was apparently well-liked, for there were many people mourning his death. Someone informed Jesus that Lazarus had been in the tomb for four days.

I couldn't help but think Jesus had really missed this one, especially after telling the three men at the river that Lazarus' illness would not end in death. I suspected they would not be welcoming Jesus with open arms.

About that time a weeping woman came running up to Jesus and threw her arms around him.

Between sobs she said, "Lord, if you had been here, my brother would not have died, but even now I know whatever you ask of God, He will give you."

The woman was Martha, and what she said made me feel terrible. I can only imagine what it did to Jesus. He told her, "Your brother will rise."

"I know he will rise, in the resurrection on the last day," she replied.

Jesus stood up straight, put his hands on Martha's shoulders and said, "I am the resurrection and the life; whoever believes in me, even if he dies will live, and everyone who lives and believes in me will never die. Do you believe this?"

She didn't hesitate for a moment. "Yes Lord, I have come to believe you are the Messiah, the Son of God, the one who is coming into the world."

After she had said this the Master's face lit up, telling me that what she had proclaimed was the truth, or that Jesus liked being referred to as the Messiah. He had that same look when he asked me who I thought he was and I answered, "The Christ, the son of the living God."

As far as I was concerned, everything Jesus had done pointed toward him being the long-awaited Messiah. However, I couldn't help wondering if the Messiah was to be sent from God, how could he have been raised in Nazareth? I was not sure, but I believe the scriptures simply say that the Messiah will be a king in the line of David. Could he not be born and raised in Nazareth? I understood how the Jewish leaders could become confused, because I was too. What I couldn't understand was their hatred for Jesus. Whoever Jesus was, whether he was the Messiah, a great prophet or just a holy man, there was no justification for hating him.

Martha had not been gone long when another distraught young woman came to Jesus and fell, crying, at his feet. It was Martha's sister Mary. Jesus helped her to her feet, and she said, "Lord, if you had been here my brother would not have died."

I silently agreed with both of them. If Jesus had left when they first came to him at the river Jordan, all of this could have been avoided.

As Jesus looked at Mary, who was still sobbing and at all of the weeping friends who had followed her, he became visibly upset, to the point of shedding tears. He asked, "Where have you laid him?"

"Sir, come and see," they exclaimed.

As we made our way towards the tomb, I could hear some of the followers talking about how much Jesus must have loved him, yet others said, "Could not this one who has given sight to the blind have done something so that Lazarus would not have died?"

I suppose he could have done that, but surely Jesus couldn't rid the world of death. They weren't being very realistic to think he could come along and stop every person from dying. Grief does strange things to a person's mind; often causing them to think and say things they ordinarily wouldn't.

When we arrived at the tomb, Jesus asked that the stone be rolled away from the entrance. Martha immediately objected, saying, "Lord, he has been dead for four days; surely there will be a stench."

It had been unusually hot the last couple of weeks, and I was positive she had a point. No one would want to get a face full of whatever was behind that stone.

Jesus said to her, "Did I not tell you that if you believe you would see the glory of God?"

The six men it took to move the stone looked at each other and then to Martha, who gave the hand gesture to roll away the stone.

Once the stone was removed, Jesus looked to heaven and said, "Father, I thank you for hearing me. I know that you always hear me, but because of the crowd here I have said this, that they may believe that you sent me."

Jesus was the only one close to the entrance, because everyone else feared the odor would be unbearable. He cried out in a loud voice, "Lazarus, come out!"

What happened next jolted my very soul and caused some among the onlookers to faint. There appeared in the doorway of the tomb a man tied hand and foot with burial bands, his face still wrapped in a cloth.

Jesus instructed them, "Untie him and let him go."

When the wrappings were removed, it was indeed the man called Lazarus.

What we had just witnessed put everything I had seen up until this point a distant second.

The little girl he had raised from the dead had only just died and I, along with everyone else, could have cited no proof that she was actually dead. But this man had died, been prepared and placed in the tomb, where he had been for four days. No one could deny the fact that the man Lazarus truly had been dead.

I had gone back and forth in coming to grips with who Jesus really was, but no more. This miracle could only have come from God.

CHAPTER 18

THE RESURRECTION OF LAZARUS SENT people in all directions screaming about the glory of God and shouting at the top of their voices that Jesus truly was the Messiah, the Son of God.

Andrew turned to me and asked, "How long do you think it will take for this story to get to Jerusalem?"

"As fast as the fastest man in the crowd can run, I expect. Maybe this will put an end to this continuous attack by the Pharisees and chief priests."

We stayed there in Bethany for a couple of days and then headed for a place called Ephraim, which was out near the desert. I could not figure out why we would retreat to such an out-of-the-way place. I really wanted to go to Jerusalem and see how differently they were going to treat Jesus since the news of Lazarus had been announced, but Jesus didn't show any interest in going anywhere. As a matter of fact, he seemed withdrawn and somewhat distant, praying for longer periods than normal.

For once, I didn't welcome the distance from the crowds. The miracle in Bethany could be the one that put Jesus over the top and closer to his kingdom. After all, it was that kingdom that we all were looking forward to, maybe even the reason we all stayed on with the teacher all these years. But whatever different reasons had led us to start this journey, every disciple was now confident we were in the presence of greatness.

It would be extremely difficult to put into words the change my life had taken, living with Jesus and actually seeing the miracles that he had worked not just once, but thousands of times.

It wasn't like Jesus to stay away from teaching for very long and the Passover was approaching. There was a rumor circulating that an admirer of Jesus within the Sanhedrin had gotten word that they were plotting to kill him. Maybe that was why Jesus was staying away from Jerusalem, although threats and danger had never stopped him before. In truth, he had been persecuted for almost all of the time I had been with him. Why they would want to kill anyone capable of doing the things Jesus had done was beyond me. It made no sense, unless it was for their personal benefit.

Of course, the obvious reason the temple leaders would want to stop Jesus from establishing his kingdom was that they knew they would be left out of the circle. Jesus had made it perfectly clear how he felt about their self-serving manipulation of the scripture. Envy can be a very dangerous thing, causing men to do unthinkable acts in an effort to stay in a seat of prominence.

As we sat around the morning fire, Jesus called two of the disciples over and gave them instructions. "Go into the city. There you will meet a man carrying a water jar, follow him. Wherever he enters, say to the master of the house, 'The teacher says, where is my guest room where I may eat the Passover with my disciples?' Then he will show you a large upper room, furnished and ready. Make the preparations for us there."

I didn't know how everyone else felt, but I was overjoyed to know we were heading back to civilization, even though that meant crowds. I was tired of the quietness of the desert town.

I never thought I would say I missed the people, but I had grown accustomed to them always being there and their absence took away from our existence.

One thing about the desert that annoyed me was the absence of smells. For most of my life I had been greeted every morning by the aromas of life by the sea—of fish-stained sorting boards on an aging boat, of fires cooking last night's catch and, when the breeze was right, olive orchards in bloom. Even today, after years away from fishing, just the slightest hint of sea air and I'm right back on my boat as if I never missed a day.

We traveled to Bethany, where Jesus had raised his friend from the dead, and stayed for a few days. The welcome Jesus received in that town was lavish, but definitely well-deserved. Why, he had brought back from the dead one of their friends, a man well-liked by everyone.

We were invited to a big dinner celebration for Jesus at the home of Martha and Mary. While eating, I noticed Lazarus reclining at the table. I wanted to ask him so many questions but decided to wait for a more appropriate time. You would have thought he would have been the center of conversation. After all, he was the reason for the celebration, yet no one mentioned it.

Mary came and sat at the Master's feet. She began bathing them in an expensive perfume and wiping them dry with her hair. Even I could tell an expensive perfume from a cheaper one. The lush aroma filled the house in minutes.

Suddenly all the quiet talk was interrupted by someone I would have least expected. Judas stood up and said, "Why has this perfume been wasted? It could have been sold for three hundred days' wages and given to the poor."

Jesus rebuked him, saying, "Leave her alone. Let her keep this for the day of my burial. The poor will be with you always, but you will not always have me."

What in the world would make Judas say something like that? He always kept the group's money bag, and I sometimes wondered how much he could be trusted. Was he really concerned about the well-being of the poor, or did he see the potential for personal gain? In our years with Jesus, I'd never noticed Judas going out of his way to minister to the poor, yet now he felt it necessary to stand up at a dinner and chastise that woman for using her own perfume. Strange indeed.

As much as Judas' behavior bothered me, Jesus's statements that he would not be with us always and that Mary could use the perfume for his burial really got me upset. After years of preaching the good news about his kingdom, why was he now obsessed with his own death? Several times Jesus had alluded to his death, even making it a point to quote the prophets. Each time, he said, "I will be handed over by the chief priests and scribes to the Gentiles and be killed."

Although I realized we couldn't possibly run and hide forever, not that Jesus would ever do such a thing, surely we could go to places that accepted what Jesus taught and proclaimed. I knew we could slip into Jerusalem unnoticed and celebrate the Passover and leave just as quietly.

While I was thinking that, there was a commotion outside and word got to us inside that a large crowd of Jews had come to see Lazarus. The word among the crowd was that the chief priests wanted Lazarus dead along with Jesus, because his resurrection was causing the crowds to believe in Jesus and that was something they were not going to stand for. That bunch of religious leaders was making Jesus, quite possibly the Messiah, a target of their envy and hateful plans. I'm not going to pretend I wasn't frightened by all that talk, but I had told myself if it got down to it, I would do everything in my power to protect Jesus and myself.

Somewhere in the past I saw myself getting old and teaching my sons how to fish, letting them do most of the work while I supplied the knowledge. Now that fishing was a distant thought, I had a hard time seeing myself in my old age. Would that kingdom come to pass? Could Jesus survive the barrage of hate that seemed to grow more evil every day? I couldn't figure out how we had gotten to this point. I believed I was with the greatest man who had ever lived, yet I couldn't have been more afraid had I been traveling in the company of the most sought-after criminal.

Still, I had hope. I hoped that when we got to Jerusalem the nightmare that had stalked us for nearly three years would be put to rest. Surely, there were some Jewish leaders who would see the great miracles Jesus had performed and realize he was, at the very least, a holy man and a great prophet. As of yet that hadn't happened, but I had hope that things would be different during the Passover.

CHAPTER 19

JERUSALEM AT PASSOVER, WHAT A glorious sight! People are coming from every region of the earth to get together and celebrate the greatest liberation of enslaved people the world had ever known. And it all had been done without armies or battles, victory was won simply by the will of God. It was one of the oldest celebration rituals in our Jewish culture.

From a distance we could see the caravans of people entering the city from all directions. Surely Jesus and our small group could enter without even raising an eyebrow.

That would not be the case, however, for as we neared the city as many as one thousand people had already gathered and was waiting for us. They were laying palm branches and their cloaks on the road as Jesus made his way into the city. To make matters worse, they were chanting and singing praises at the tops of their voices. Now we stuck out like a sore thumb, causing more and more onlookers to crowd around to see who it was that was making such a grand entrance.

"Hosanna! Hosanna in the highest!" the crowds shouted over and over. They might as well have been ringing a dinner bell calling the pack of evildoers who were on the prowl for Jesus.

On the positive side, I had always believed there is safety in numbers. As far as I could tell at that moment, the numbers were certainly in our favor.

Although it appeared that the tide was no longer against us, something kept nagging at my gut. How would the chief priests and their cronies feel about all the attention Jesus was receiving? That was the very reason they were set on killing Jesus and Lazarus. Now we were marching right into Jerusalem, practically daring them to make the next move.

To make matters worse, Jesus was riding a colt two disciples had brought back from a nearby town at the Master's request. While he did look like a king making his way into the city, that was not how I envisioned us arriving at the feast, and I was positive everyone at the temple knew we were here.

Time would tell how all this would be received and I still hoped that when the people of Jerusalem knew the truth about Jesus raising Lazarus from the dead, they would see him in a whole new light.

Things picked up right where they had left off, with the multitudes of pushing and shoving people trying desperately to get Jesus to acknowledge them in hopes of being healed or just to say they touched the man. Although the excitement was beyond anything I could have imagined Jesus seemed to be not nearly as caught up in the moment as I was.

As far as I was concerned things couldn't have started any better. If Jesus was going to establish a new kingdom, we were starting off on the right foot. It was easy to tell when Jesus was distracted; his focus would never be on any one person. Instead, he would look right through the pressing crowds as if they weren't there.

Rather than reacting to the joyous welcome with approval and excitement, Jesus' face seemed etched in stone with an expression more suitable for a funeral than a coronation.

"Master, it appears you have found favor with the people of Jerusalem," I yelled, trying my best to be heard. He turned to me, saying, "These people are like reeds in the wind, bending where the wind is the strongest. Remember, glory is always fleeting."

I could not help but think what will it take? What has to happen before Jesus realizes that the crowd is his for the taking?

Jesus had talked about setting up his kingdom for as long as I had been with him, and yet when the opportunity presented itself to launch this new kingdom, his interest seemed to wane. If Jesus were to rise to a position of power, I believed it would have to start with an overzealous crowd and continue to build until the Romans could no longer keep the Jewish nation under their thumb. Then the twelve of us could rule the twelve tribes of Israel with Jesus as our king, just as he promised.

I would be lying if I said this wasn't a strong motivation for my staying with Jesus, but it would be just as wrong to ignore all the other marvelous reasons I was still with him. I just wished Jesus would take action and set up his kingdom as soon as possible. That way we could stop traveling all over Judea telling everyone about the good news and start living it.

In the city, the activities surrounding the feast

of the Passover took on a different tone. As usual, there were the multitudes of people and the constant banter of merchants and buyers. But this time we seemed to be the focus of attention, and I was sure it had everything to do with our royal welcoming party.

In the distance I could see spies for the temple taking in everything so they could give an accurate report back to the Pharisees and priests. I knew the chief priest and his minions were probably fuming with anger over the way Jesus was being adored and idolized, but the things Jesus had done simply demanded that kind of response, and they were just going to have to deal with it. I knew that with the feast of the Passover and all the crowds we were about as safe as we could get, and my tension eased a bit.

Finding a place to stay during Passover was always difficult. Each year, thousands of people would overflow the city, forcing them to set up their tents outside the city walls as makeshift homes for the feast. I knew we had a place to celebrate our Passover meal, but I had no idea where we would find lodging, given there was none to be had. Possibly someone in the crowd would invite the Master and us to stay with them as had been the case for most of our journey. It really didn't matter where we ended up; I was looking forward to the twelve of us sharing the Passover meal with the Master as part of such a marvelous feast.

Although there were multitudes of people around us, I noticed Judas was nowhere to be found. What would prompt a man who appeared to be scared of his own shadow to venture off alone, knowing the situation we were in? Maybe like me, he felt the safety of the numbers or possibly he thought he would go unnoticed. I asked about his whereabouts, but no one had a clue. James said, "Ask the teacher, maybe he sent him on a mission." I asked Jesus, but instead of answering he gave me a look that was more perplexing than the man himself.

Judas' absence concerned me. Maybe he had been abducted and was being held against his will. Deep down, however, my greatest concern was his true loyalty to Jesus and the other eleven of us.

CHAPTER 20

B EING HEMMED IN BY ALL the crowds blocked a lot of the breeze, so we made our way to a shaded area to sit and refresh ourselves. The temperature difference was most delightful.

Suddenly Andrew and Phillip made their way to Jesus from the back of the crowd with some Greeks who had asked to meet Jesus.

Jesus stood up and said, "The hour has come for the Son of Man to be glorified. Amen, amen, I say to you, unless a grain of wheat falls to the ground and dies, it remains just a grain of wheat; but if it dies it produces much fruit. Whoever loves his life will lose it, and whoever hates his life in this world will preserve it for eternal life. Whoever serves me must follow me, and where I am, there also will my servant be. The father will honor whoever serves me. I am troubled now, yet what should I say? 'Father, save me from this hour'? But it was for this purpose that I came to this hour. Father, glorify thy name."

As if in response, a loud voice said, "I have glorified it and will glorify it again."

The people were startled and argued among themselves. Some said it was thunder; while others said an angel had spoken. I heard the noise and it definitely wasn't thunder. Thunder rumbles; it doesn't sound out words, and the words had been clearly heard. As the people in the crowd debated, Jesus quelled the argument by saying, "That voice did not come for my sake but for yours. Now is the time of judgment on the world; now the ruler of this world will be driven out and when I am lifted up from the earth I will draw everyone to myself."

I was not sure what Jesus meant, but it wasn't the first time my imagination fell short, and I was sure Jesus would explain it to all of us. Over the years I had come to know that if there was something I did not understand, whether I mentioned it or not, Jesus would make sure I fully understood what he intended.

As I think back, I realized that he never let anyone walk away misunderstanding him, except for the time he told the multitudes he would give them his flesh to eat. They walked away shaking their heads in disbelief, and Jesus never did explain what he really meant. Obviously, he could not give them his flesh to eat or his blood to drink, yet he watched one of the largest crowds of people leave at one time without any attempt to explain that bizarre teaching.

The voice we all heard responded to Jesus' request almost immediately, just as the storm did on the Sea of Galilee. Jesus was obviously more than a holy man or any prophet I had ever heard of. But for a man with so much power he was as timid as a lamb, never wanting to push his beliefs on anyone.

In fact, he was the most unlikely king I had ever seen. Kings didn't tell you what to believe and then leave it up to you to accept it or not. No sir, they demanded it. That was the character flaw I saw in Jesus which I believed might prevent him from ever sitting on a throne. He did show a lot of leadership and spunk when he drove the money lenders out of the temple, but such a display of authority was rare. Of course, I was hoping that I was wrong for if Jesus never comes into his kingdom, none of us would ever rule over the twelve tribes of Israel, and speaking for myself, that was something I was looking forward to. I had to be patient, trusting everything Jesus said. After all, he had proven time and again to be more trustworthy than anyone I had ever known.

The evening came, and we made our way to the house where we were to have our Passover meal. The man showed us to an upper room that was large and spacious, complete with everything needed for our celebration meal. Because of the low ceiling the air in the room was heavy with smoke from the lamps. As we removed our sandals, Jesus motioned each one of us over.

He had a towel around his waist and began washing each man's feet. I watched in absolute amazement, wondering what in the world had gotten into our Master. If anything, we should be washing his feet, not the other way around.

When it was my turn, I wasted no time telling Jesus there was no way I would allow my Master to wash my feet! While I thought he would appreciate my gesture, I was shocked when once again he rebuked me saying, "Unless I wash your feet, you will have no inheritance with me."

I didn't know what washing my feet could have to do with my inheritance, but if washing my feet was necessary, "then wash my head and hands as well," I insisted.

Jesus said there was no need to be washed all over but that one among us was not clean.

"Who are you referring to and why is he not clean," I asked.

Jesus never gave me an answer, rather he put his garments back on and again reclined at the table.

While we listened, he told us he had given us a model to follow. If the teacher and master could wash our feet, then we should do likewise. I thought I had understood his teaching in the past—how it was important to never put ourselves above others, keeping us grounded with love for one another—but this was much more dramatic. I was not smart enough to understand how such logic would serve a king, but I could see how it would change the way everyone got along.

That was yet another reason why seeing Jesus as a king was difficult. A king would never wash another man's feet or lower himself into the service of another, yet that was exactly what Jesus said was necessary. Looking around the table at the others' faces in the glow of the lamps, I was sure I was not alone in my lack of understanding.

I was beginning to think this kingdom would be very different than any I was familiar with. It would be more like a brotherhood of men with Jesus as the leader, and I was all right with that. It just wasn't unfolding the way Jesus described it. As I looked at the faces of the other men gathered around the table, I saw questions and doubt as to where all this would lead us.

Andrew talked to me all the time, often asking the same question, "Brother, what will happen to us should something ever befall the Teacher?"

"Nothing will happen to Jesus," I would reassure him, all the while knowing I needed an answer to the same question. Sometimes I would tease my brother and say, "They haven't moved the sea since we left. Have you forgotten how to fish?"

"No, but the Master has promised us so much more, I kind of hoped to never pull in another net, if that's all right with you," he'd say with that sheepish grin.

I did recall Jesus saying, "I will make you fishers of men," but Jesus seemed to be the only one catching any.

CHAPTER 21

J ESUS STOOD UP AT THE center of the long table holding the Passover feast. "I am not referring to all of you," he said, "I know those I have chosen. But the scripture will be fulfilled, 'The one who shares my bread has raised his heel against me.' I am telling you this now, so when it happens you will believe that I am The One. I say to you, whoever receives The One I send receives me, and whoever receives me receives The One who sent me."

Jesus sat back down, but his face told me that something was still heavy on his mind.

There was nothing unusual about Jesus teaching us while we ate; he did so nearly every evening. If the matter troubling him was something he felt we needed to hear, it would be said. Personally, I hoped it wasn't something that would ruin our Passover meal, but I sensed we were about to hear something unpleasant. I hoped it wasn't about his death.

The reason that came to mind was his demeanor had been about the same on several other occasions when he had told us of his impending arrest and death, and that was definitely some news I could go without hearing.

After carefully scanning every face around him, Jesus lowered his head and looking down at the table said something that devastated me, and I am quite sure the rest of the men around the table.

"Amen, amen, I say to you, one of you will betray me."

"What? Who in this room would betray you," I blurted out, just before the entire room exploded with the same question. All around the table, the men were looking cautiously at one another and shaking their heads in disbelief or denial.

John was at Jesus' right side, so I gave him a look and nod, hoping to prod him to ask Jesus for the name of the betrayer. John leaned in and asked Jesus something, which I could only assume was, "Who is it?" He received a response, but I couldn't hear it.

That was the first time my anger had reached such a level in many years, and for some reason my eyes locked onto Judas. He was the only man in the room who appeared not to be in shock. On the contrary, he seemed amazed. Was his puzzled look because he had been exposed as a traitor in front of his friends, because Jesus knew about it, or both?

Of course, I didn't know for sure that it was Judas, but as soon as I could get closer to John I would find out what Jesus had told him.

Jesus dipped some bread into the dish and handed it to Judas, saying, "What you are going to do, do quickly."

Had I been wrong? In my mind, I was convinced that Judas was the traitor, so why would Jesus send him on an errand? Indeed, why would he send anyone out at this hour, in the middle of our Passover meal when everyone in the city was indoors?

Judas did in fact leave, and the rest of us continued questioning one another, trying desperately to find out which man Jesus had been talking about. It wasn't until later that John shared the answer Jesus had given him: "It is the one to whom I hand the bread after I have dipped it."

Why did Jesus allow Judas to leave before we knew it was him? I could not understand the reasoning behind his logic. Had he told us it was Judas, I swear that man never would have made it out of the room. Now, he was out doing the kind of business I had always suspected he was capable of, but more than that, he could make our whereabouts known to the people who were our greatest threat.

I wondered if it was the fact that one of his closest friends was going to betray him, or the consequences that might follow that had Jesus in such a somber mood.

Since none of us knew of Judas's intentions, we went on with the Passover meal. Jesus took the bread, said a blessing and broke it. He then gave a piece to each of us, saying, "This is my body, take and eat."

When every man had eaten his portion, he took the cup of wine, blessed it and said, "Take this, all of you, and drink from it. This cup is my blood, the blood of the new and everlasting covenant. It will be shed for you and for many for the forgiveness of sins. Do this in memory of me."

I ate and drank just as I was instructed, but I couldn't help but think of the time he told the multitude he was going to give them his body and blood to eat and drink. Was this the moment he had been referring to, or did his words have a deeper meaning? If he had been referring to this ceremony his words now made perfect sense. On the other hand, if it were so simple, why wouldn't he have explained it to the people before they walked away? No, he had been much more inflexible in his answers, not willing to budge on that day.

I was sure his teaching on that day related to today, but if it were as simple as the bread and wine symbolizing his body and blood he would have made that clear, but he didn't.

When the Passover meal was over Jesus said, "Let us go to the Mount of Olives to pray." As we made our way along, Jesus referenced the scriptures saying, "This night all of you will have your faith in me shaken, for it is written: 'I will strike the shepherd, and the sheep of the flock will be dispersed.' But after I have been raised up, I shall go before you to Galilee."

"I don't know about the rest of these men, but I will never lose my faith in you!" I snapped.

Jesus turned to me with a look of disappointment and said, "Amen, I say to you, Cephas, this very night before the cock crows, you will deny me three times."

I felt a shock wave go through my body, chilling me to the core. "Never!" was the first thing that came out of my mouth. "What kind of man do you think I am? Even if I have to die with you, I will never deny you!" Immediately all of the other men chimed in their agreement.

I whispered to James and John, "If we are in jeopardy, why head to the Mount of Olives? Let us take this opportunity to slip away in the night and avoid whatever Jesus is talking about."

I was quite sure God would hear his prayers from any place Jesus chose to pray. The further away from here the better, was my plan.

What in the world was Judas up to? If he was going to betray Jesus then he was betraying us too. I didn't think Jesus was thinking that through; we were headed to pray where he always prayed, and Judas knew exactly where that was.

We reached a place where Jesus told everyone except John, James and me to rest and pray. He motioned for the three of us to follow him. After making our way to the area called the Garden of Gethsemane, Jesus instructed us to stay alert, watch and pray.

Pondering what Jesus had said left me empty. I sat there with James and John, unable to focus on prayer, hoping what Jesus had predicted never came to pass. At the same time, I couldn't recall a single time when he said something was going to happen and it didn't. I just kept telling myself that the only way Jesus' terrible prediction could happen was if I allowed it, and that was something I refused to accept.

CHAPTER 22

A MAN HAS ONLY A FEW things he can take to the grave with him and loyalty to a friend tops the list. Jesus wasn't just a friend, he was possibly the Messiah and at the very least, a magnificent prophet and tremendous holy man. Whatever he might be, he was definitely Israel's best chance to gain independence, possibly overthrowing Rome. I realized that for that to happen he would have to make peace with the religious leaders, if that was still possible. However, if he walked blindly into the grasp of those self-righteous vipers then I was certain they would manipulate the powers that be, causing everyone who would listen to believe he was a threat to Israel instead of their savior. If they accomplished that, anything could happen.

The tables had been turned on me quickly. One minute I was ready to beat Judas unmercifully for doing the unthinkable, the next I had been told I would deny my beloved Master not just once, but three times. The accusation was a solid kick in the gut, and I was determined to never let it happen.

Jesus moved a short distance away from us, falling to his knees as he began to pray. We could hear most of what he was saying; he sounded very distressed. It wasn't his everyday prayers we were accustomed to hearing. Rather he was asking God, whom he addressed as his Father, to take the cup away if it were possible. However, he insisted that as much as he wanted that prayer answered, what he wanted more was that it be his Father's will instead of his own.

I never saw Jesus in a state like this; he was shaking and sweating profusely as if his very life was at stake. It was very hard for me to watch, all the while feeling completely helpless.

"Maybe we should be with him," John whispered. "After all, we are the only comfort he has."

"No, he told us to wait here and be watchful and pray. That is exactly what we should do," I reminded them.

The main reason I wanted to stay put stemmed from the fear and anxiety welling up inside of me. That was a weakness I didn't want to share with the others. It was bad enough that Jesus, the center of our world, was in a state of absolute distress, but if the others knew how unsettled I was becoming, who would they look to for strength? Although the rest of the group was a short distance away and unable to witness what the three of us saw and heard, it wouldn't take long for this information to change hands and I didn't want to be thought of as weak.

With all these thoughts swirling around in my head I must have dozed off, because the next thing I knew Jesus was standing over us, asking why we could not stay awake with him and pray for only an hour. I didn't know the exact time but it was late in the night, and we had put in a long day. Keeping awake wasn't easy. We agreed to keep each other awake and do as Jesus asked as he returned to the same spot and resumed his anguished prayer.

Try as I might, remaining awake escaped me as well as the others, resulting in Jesus having to awaken us again. I could tell he was definitely more perturbed with us this time, leading him to address us more sternly than before.

"Watch and pray, that you may not fail the test," he pleaded. "The spirit is willing, but the flesh is weak."

I was ashamed to answer him. He was asking for so little and we were unable to deliver. I looked at Jesus closely. His hair was soaked with sweat and the drops that fell appeared to be mixed with blood as they stained his garments on his chest and shoulders. How could anyone pray with that kind of intensity, and what did it mean?

He left us once again to resume his prayers, leaving us with similar instructions to remain awake. Try as I might, the harder I fought to stay awake the quicker sleep came, leaving us in the same position Jesus had found us in two times already. I never heard him return but he shook me, saying, "Get up, the time has come for the Son of Man to be given over to the powers of darkness and sinners. Let us go. See, my betrayer is at hand."

In the distance I could see a large group approaching with swords and clubs. In the light of the torches it was easy to make out the image of Judas leading the way. He had done exactly what Jesus predicted he would do. Making the decision to come here and pray was a bad choice, just as I had predicted. The mob consisted of mostly temple guards along with a few of the more radical temple officials there to make sure their prey didn't escape.

I looked right at Judas but he kept his head down, avoiding any eye contact. I wanted so badly to grab him and demand to know how he could do such an evil thing. In the midst of all the commotion I hadn't noticed that the rest of the disciples had gathered around Jesus, acting as a human shield.

Leaving the mob, Judas walked right by John and embraced Jesus, saying "Hail, Rabbi," and kissed him on the cheek. Had I been Jesus, I would have slugged him right then and there.

Instead, Jesus asked him, "Judas, are you betraying the Son of Man with a kiss?"

Immediately the guards in the front stepped forward to grab hold of him. My mind was swirling, as it became difficult to breathe and I couldn't decide what to do. Then it became crystal clear to me. I was going to kill Judas for what he had done and then protect Jesus from this mob of evildoers.

I pulled my sword from its scabbard and lunged in the direction of Judas, who had turned his back and was walking away. I made a hard slash, but someone bumped into me, whether intentional or due to the scuffle that was occurring as they tried to arrest Jesus I didn't know. The encounter sent my sword in a wayward direction. Instead of hitting my target, I ended up slicing off the ear of one of the temple guards. Before I could draw back my sword for another attempt, three other guards grabbed me and wrestled me to the ground.

I had lost all sense of fear, and I'm not sure if I was fighting for Jesus or to save myself, but I heard Jesus yell.

"Enough!" he said. "Put away your sword. All who live by the sword will perish by the sword. Do you think I cannot call upon my Father and He will provide me with twelve legions of angels in a moment? But, then, how would the scriptures be fulfilled that say it must come to pass this way?"

He then addressed the church officials and guards. "Have you come out as against a robber, with swords and clubs to arrest me? Day after day I sat teaching in the temple area, yet you did not arrest me. But all this has come to pass that the writings of the prophets may be fulfilled."

Things were happening so fast, yet I saw Jesus bend down, pick up the severed ear and miraculously reattach it to the man's head. Here we were at the precipice of our demise, we were going to be killed, either here or after being paraded in front of the high priest, and yet Jesus was performing a miracle for his adversary. I wondered if I would ever be capable of such love and compassion, not only for my brothers, but as Jesus taught us, for my enemies.

How was that possible? The only thing I wanted at that moment was more men so we could turn back this aggression that was initiated by the very people who should have been embracing Jesus, not treating him like a common criminal.

Fear will do one of two things to a man; either the person will rise to the challenge, getting control of the situation or he will cower in shame and succumb to the fear. I didn't feel like I had failed the test, but as I wrestled with the guards I wondered if I was giving my best effort. After all, I knew if I were to regain my footing there was a good chance one of those guards would remember that I took a slash at one of their own. That might cause him to get nervous and draw his own sword.

There was shouting as men were either fighting or running for their lives, yet there in the midst of it all stood Jesus, looking neither frightened nor angry, but perfectly calm.

In only minutes Jesus and I had been surrounded and overtaken by this gang of cowards. They had bound his hands and feet, but the thing that sickened me most was the sound of men's fists as they landed with horrifying thuds against the face and body of my friend.

Thinking about the kind of man it takes to punch and beat a helpless man who is bound and unable to defend himself caused my anger to surge. Yet, given the opportunity I wasn't sure Jesus would defend himself, even if they set him free. Again, the fire inside of me reached a point where watching and not doing everything I could was worse than dying.

I remember fighting with all the strength I could muster. Just as I was about to get to my feet, my head felt like it was split in two. The starlit sky went black.

CHAPTER 23

I WOKE WITH A POUNDING HEAD, surrounded by olive trees and darkness. As I staggered to my feet my eyes were unable to focus. Eventually I could make out the light from the torches as the procession made its way down the Mount of Olives. Although I knew I had been knocked unconscious; I knew it hadn't been for very long.

Where were all the others, I wondered as I stumbled in the dark with legs that were still not very steady. I knew my efforts fell short of heroic, but at least I had made an attempt, which was more than could be said for any of the others. It was easy to be critical of the others; they weren't there to defend themselves and I wasn't about to judge myself too harshly.

As I made my way down the mountain, my head began to clear. It still hurt from the blow I had received, but I began to feel the nerves and fear come alive again. Most of the fear was of the unknown. What would happen to Jesus? What would happen to all of us? What about the kingdom and the twelve seats we were to occupy? Of course, there would be only eleven now that Judas had sold us out.

As I began to think about those things, my mind went back to when Jesus said he would be handed over to the priests and would suffer and die. Well, he had been handed over and Jesus was definitely suffering. I fell to my knees. Please God, I prayed, spare his life, if for no other reason than to continue his teaching and healing.

It's funny how a man looks back on his life with the clarity of a crystal; it has many facets but it takes each one to form a beautiful stone. When we began our journey nothing made sense and the crowds had a way of driving me mad. Now, I would have traded ten years of my life just to go back to that day when we left the boat with such hope, wonder and anticipation.

If my time with Jesus had taught me anything, it had shown me that men cannot be trusted and a day can go from joyous to disastrous at a moment's notice. It certainly had today.

I could tell I was catching up with the arresting party, not only from the sound of wildly violent men but from the smell of burning torches that filled the night air.

"Take him to Caiaphas," they continually shouted.

Of all the places for them to take Jesus, the house of the high priest would have been my last choice, but in my heart I had the feeling that the visit would come as no surprise to Caiaphas. In fact, he was probably expecting it.

I realized the mob had arrived just minutes ahead of me because the courtyard of the high priest was buzzing with news about the arrest of Jesus. Some were stunned and shocked by the way he was being treated, yet none of them dared make their way into the house of Caiaphas to testify in his defense.

I scanned the crowd for friendly faces and found none. I moved closer to the fire in an effort to not only warm myself, but perhaps get a feel for how the crowd was thinking.

Surely they would only question Jesus and release him. After all, what else could they do to him, especially when he had done nothing? As I watched, a steady stream of elders, members of the Sanhedrin and scribes slipped into the house of the high priest. They reminded me of rats creeping into a grain house, hoping to get their fill.

As I watched, the chatter was broken by the voice of a woman saying, "You too were with Jesus the Galilean."

I looked around as if she might have been talking to someone else, but in the glow of the fire, everyone's eyes were fixed on me.

"I don't even know the man you are talking about. You must have mistaken me for someone else," I answered quickly. I wasn't sure if everyone believed me, but they seemed to return to their own business and conversation.

That was more attention than I needed, especially coming on the heels of what had just taken place in the garden. I decided I should find another vantage point from where I could watch the proceedings, one that was a little safer. I got up and headed toward a large tree in the corner of the courtyard that was away from the firelight.

Before I could make it to the safety of the shadows, a young maid pointed at me and said, "This man was with Jesus the Nazarene."

I swallowed hard, trying to compose myself and

look as indignant as possible. "I swear I do not know the man. You are mistaken."

It was bad enough I was lying, but the looks I was getting from the crowd in the courtyard had begun to scare me. I thought it was time to make myself scarce and head for the gate so as not to make myself a target.

Suddenly a man put his hand on my shoulder and turned me around. "Surely you are one of them," he said, his eyes searching my face. "Even your speech gives you away."

I don't know what got into me. I started cursing and swearing, "No! I don't know the man! Now, leave me be!" I wrenched free of his grasp.

Now I knew what a young sheep felt like when he was surrounded by a pack of hungry wolves. I admit I was terrified, not wanting to be attacked and dragged into the house of Caiaphas.

As I hurriedly exited the courtyard, I was stopped in my tracks by the sound of a rooster crowing.

What little strength I had immediately left my legs and my knees buckled, plunging me on my face. Jesus had told me in front of everyone that, "Before the cock crows, you will deny me three times." I had told him that was rubbish and yet, when put to the test that is exactly what I had done.

I plunged into a void of darkness, where a man's failing reason can no longer keep his soul afloat. The realization that I had traded my friendship with Jesus for the mantle of coward sickened me beyond words.

As I stumbled to my feet, I wanted only solitude. I needed time and space to sort things out, but my conscience wasn't going to let me off easy. "You traitor. You're no better than that slime Judas, who brought that mob to arrest him. At least he had the guts to do it in front of everyone. You not only lied repeatedly, but you betrayed Jesus by disowning him in front of that whole crowd."

As I tried to fight off the endless assault from my own conscience, I began sobbing uncontrollably. The memory of Jesus putting out his hand when I was drowning only served to plunge the knife deeper. I had seen Jesus do hundreds of miraculous things, but I didn't know if forgiving me was something he could or would even want to do, that is, if I even had the guts to ask him.

As I made my way away from the courtyard, I could only hope none of the others had been there and heard me lie and disown Jesus. How a man could think the things I thought of Judas and then turn around and do the very same thing was beyond my comprehension. I couldn't imagine myself asking Jesus to forgive me, especially when I didn't deserve it.

Looking behind me, I saw John enter the courtyard with two women. They appeared to be Mary Magdalene and Mary, the mother of Jesus. Knowing what I had done and how it was keeping me from being there with them was almost more than I could bear.

I wandered to the outskirts of the city, looking for a place where I could be alone. Finding solitude was difficult with so many people here celebrating Passover.

At that moment, I knew only one thing: I had to

ask God for forgiveness and hope that Jesus would forgive me too. Crying like a child, I dropped to my knees and asked God for an audience. I promised if he would forgive me for my acts of cowardice, I would never again fail him in such a miserable fashion.

CHAPTER 24

PROBABLY AN HOUR HAD PASSED since the courtyard episode, and I headed back to the area, hoping they were finished questioning Jesus or whatever it was they were doing. Before reaching the high priest's house, I could hear the sound of a large number of people making their way in the opposite direction. As I hastened toward the sound, I happened on a young man heading in my direction. Noticing he was in a hurry, I asked, "What is all the commotion about?"

"They're taking him to Pilate," he answered quickly, not wanting to slow down.

"Taking who to Pilate?"

"Jesus of Nazareth!" he shot back before disappearing into the night.

Why were they taking Jesus to Pontius Pilate? I couldn't think of even one thing Jesus had done wrong, much less something that would require an audience with the governor. One thing was certain; no one wanted to visit Pilate at this hour, regardless of the reason.

Picking up the pace, I caught up with the mob making their way to see Pilate.

"What exactly is going on," I asked an older man who was falling behind.

"They found the teacher they call Jesus guilty of blasphemy and they are sending him to Pilate."

"Why Pilate? What role does a Roman governor have in a matter of Jewish Law," I inquired.

"They want to have him crucified and our Law doesn't allow it," he informed me.

Hearing the word "crucified" stopped me in my tracks. Crucifixion was something for criminals, not for Jesus. How had things gone so terribly wrong in such a short time? One minute we were praying in the Garden, the next Jesus was being dragged before a man who had no patience for such matters. A death sentence for a Jew meant nothing to Pilate. He would likely render such a judgment just so he could return to sleep.

I waded through the crowd, making sure to keep my head down so as not to be identified. When I got to where I could see Jesus, I could not believe it was the same man I had been with in the garden only hours before. He was disfigured from the punches to his face the guards had obviously continued to inflict. Roped and chained like a dangerous criminal, his body was limp as they dragged him through the streets.

I had seen many murderers executed, but none had been treated like that and they deserved their punishment. I felt the energy leave my body, so I got out of the crowd and found a place to collapse. I could only watch as I wondered: if my world was dark an hour earlier, how much more so will it be if those madmen have their way?

I had not been there long when self-preservation took over. Not fear so much, but a desire to stay alive for the others and to support Jesus in any way I could. Naturally, I thought: If they can crucify Jesus, how hard would it be to hang the rest of us on a tree? That was all the motivation I needed to keep me away from the crowds and Pilate's courtyard.

I really don't remember having a plan or deciding what to do next, but somehow I wound up at the upper room where we had eaten our Passover meal earlier that evening. It was empty now, and I had never felt more alone than at that moment. Where were the others? Although the crowd escorting Jesus was large, I had seen none of our group there.

Of course, being afraid of being pointed out it was extremely difficult to scan the crowd with my head down. I knew this fear that had gripped me had to be dealt with, but I couldn't see how getting myself in the same situation as Jesus would be of any benefit.

I needed some company and fellowship with the others, especially my brother to help sort it out, but I feared they were hiding and trying to get a handle on what had happened, just like I was.

Despite the outside dangers, staying in that house kept me from knowing the fate of Jesus, something that my future was tied to. Against all of my instincts, I ventured out into the street. I had only just left when I ran into Andrew.

My joy was only momentary as Andrew informed me that Pilate wanted nothing to do with Jesus. Instead, he sent him to see King Herod. On the one hand I was overjoyed that Jesus had escaped Pilate's wrath, but he could be in just as much danger being brought before Herod. This was the maniacal king who had John the Baptist beheaded for simply telling the truth and preaching repentance. I knew all too well if Herod looked to Jesus for answers, the answers he would get might very well bring Jesus to the same end as John.

Andrew and I agreed to mix in with the crowd, hoping to locate the others and formulate a plan of what to do if the worst happened. I felt better being nearer to Jesus, even though we were a considerable distance from Herod's palace. As much as I wanted to help him, I told myself there was nothing I could do. I was too self-focused to realize that had I been on the front line where Jesus could see me, at least he would have known I was there for him.

We had not been there long when the guards brought Jesus out and led him away. The word was that Herod thought Jesus was an imposter and was sending him back to Pilate. This nightmare just wouldn't go away. Jesus had gone before Pilate and King Herod without anything bad happening. Now he must go back and tempt fate again.

It was painfully obvious that the high priests had worked hard to obtain this arrest and were not going to just let their quarry walk away. A terrible feeling came over me about this next visit with Pilate, but regardless of the outcome I intended to be present.

I suggested to Andrew that we go back to the upper room and try to get some rest, knowing full well it would be morning before Jesus would be brought before Pilate. Sleep escaped us both as we talked. Why would Jesus, who seemed to foresee and understand everything, allow our journey and mission to come to such an abrupt halt? If there was a purpose for the tragedy that lay before us, it was far from my ability to understand. Of course, during the years we had traveled with Jesus this wasn't the first time that something happened which I didn't see a reason or have an answer for, but it was definitely the most perplexing.

Somewhere during our conversation we dozed off, only to be awakened by loud knocking at the door. I ran to the door and peeking through the cracks, I saw Phillip and James. We welcomed them in and shared only a brief reunion before James nervously said, "They are gathering in Pilate's courtyard. Are you going to go see what happens?"

"Absolutely, let us be on our way," I answered.

All the way there I found myself constantly looking behind us, expecting temple guards or Roman soldiers to be on the lookout for us. After all, they had our leader. If they got us too, their troubles would be over.

Except for the short time Andrew and I had been sent out to preach, this was the longest I had been away from Jesus, and I certainly felt his absence. Even when we were out preaching I could feel his presence, almost as if he was with us.

Upon arriving at the courtyard we learned that Jesus had been sent away to be scourged, after which Pilate would release him. How could they flog a man who by Pilate's own admission had done nothing? On the other hand, as bad as that would be, if Jesus could get by with only a flogging then maybe we could leave Jerusalem and put this nightmare far, far behind us.

The riff among the crowd was very hostile, which

led me to believe there could be a violent dispute between the Jewish elders and the followers of Jesus. Even though Jesus was being beaten, they continued to talk about crucifying him.

The Roman soldiers appeared to be getting edgy and were doing their best to quash any uprising before it could begin, while the church elders continued keeping the mob whipped into frenzy saying that Jesus' blasphemy was too great to be forgiven.

Nothing could have prepared me for the horrifying sight of Jesus when they brought him back from being flogged. I don't know if any man had ever been beaten so severely. He was practically unrecognizable. There wasn't a place on his body that had not been lacerated. He was bleeding so profusely, Pilate had some of his servants wipe up the blood from his feet as it ran and dripped from his torn flesh. Even Pilate seemed shocked by the brutality of the scourging.

The collective gasp that rippled through the crowd at the first sight of Jesus was quickly drowned out by shouts and jeering, mostly from the Jewish elders. Standing there that day and witnessing what I saw, my heart would have been moved for even the most vicious criminal. Then when I thought I couldn't be shocked any more, as Pilate announced he was going to release Jesus, the mob shouted, "Crucify him!"

"But this is your king. You would crucify your king?" Pilate asked.

"We have no king but Caesar. Crucify him!" they shouted louder.

"I find no reason to condemn this man. If he has broken your laws, then you crucify him," Pilate shouted.

They responded, "We have no law permitting us to put a man to death, but he has made himself to be God and for that he should die."

For whatever reason, the Roman governor was having a difficult time making a firm decision, taking Jesus back inside two times. It was obvious that Pilate wanted to get this over with, but he also wanted to appease Caiaphas and the high priests, knowing full well a decision against their wishes would cause civil unrest, and that would not sit well with the emperor.

To his credit, Pilate came up with a clever plan. Since it was customary for the governor to release one Jewish prisoner during the Passover festival, he gave the crowd a choice between releasing Jesus or Barabbas, a murderous fiend. He was confident the crowd would pick Jesus, thereby getting Pilate off the hook of having to crucify him. It was not because Pilate had suddenly developed a conscience or anything; but he had questioned Jesus face-to-face, and I believe he saw there was no evil in him.

You would think that under no circumstances would Barabbas be the crowd's choice to be released on the streets, but that mob was going with whatever the temple leaders wanted. "Free Barabbas!" they screamed. "Crucify Jesus!"

The chorus of voices stunned Pilate, who I am quite sure never expected his plan to turn out like that. Finally a visibly irritated Pilate stood and stated loudly, "I wash my hands of this man's death; his blood is on you."

"His blood be on us and on our children," came the crowd's reply.

Immediately Jesus was taken away to the shouts of "Crucify him!"

I wanted to do something, anything, but I knew deep inside there was absolutely nothing to be done. Jesus had been betrayed not only by Judas, but by his very own people.

CHAPTER 25

MY MIND WAS RACING, TRYING to understand not only what was about to happen but what would become of us. I knew now that the kingdom Jesus talked about would never come. We would be left to fend for ourselves, all the while doing our best to stay unnoticed and alive.

I already knew there was no way I could watch them crucify Jesus, but Andrew and James felt differently. "We have to be there; he's all alone," Andrew pointed out.

"It would only mean trouble for us, and we could never get close enough for the master to know we were even there. Besides, how could you two possibly look at Jesus nailed to a cross?" I questioned them. No, I believed it was in our best interest to go back to the house, gather with the others and wait for everything to blow over.

"I'm scared too Peter ... but hiding? What would Jesus want us to do?" Andrew whispered, trying to mask the fear in his voice.

"I don't know what Jesus would expect us to do, but I am certain of one thing, whatever it is, we certainly can't do it in prison or worse, nailed to a tree." With as much authority as I could muster I told them, "We need to gather and come up with a plan, and we can't do that by ducking around the streets, trying to go unnoticed."

I didn't need to beg them to go along with my plan because deep in their hearts they knew it was our best chance to survive this catastrophic turn of events, which seemed to end the glorious ride we had been on for the last three years.

I thought about what Andrew had asked, "What would Jesus want us to do?" For the life of me I couldn't come up with an answer. Surely the Master hadn't spent all those years teaching us, just to have them end here. Questions swirled in my head, questions that only Jesus himself could answer.

Most of us had locked ourselves in the house where we had shared our last meal with Jesus when there was a loud knock on the door. Looking at one another, we all expected the other to go see who it was. When no one moved, I got to my feet and the crack in the door enabled me to see Matthew outside. I opened the door, and Matthew shot inside much quicker than I could get the door closed behind him.

"It was awful," he sobbed. "Absolutely horrible. He's nearly dead now; they've killed our Lord."

"Did you see any of the others there?" I probed.

"Yes," said Matthew. "I saw John with Mary and Jesus' mother. They were standing at the foot of the cross, close enough to touch it."

Knowing what Andrew and James must be thinking caused a wave of shame to well up in me. They had the guts to go to the crucifixion and I talked them out of it. Not only them, I talked myself out of it too.

I had never been more confused and scared. I

was terrified of what this would do, not only to me but to all of the men and women who had given their very lives to this man Jesus. Now we were in limbo—no Jesus, no direction, and years removed from the only life we had known.

***

Suddenly a strange darkness came over the land, not like the dark of night but a darkness so black you could actually feel it. What made it even more strange was that it wasn't quite mid-afternoon, and the absence of wind or rain made it all the more eerie.

"What's going on?" several voices asked at once.

"I don't know," snapped Matthew. "There wasn't a cloud in the sky and sunset is not for several hours and yet it's black as night."

I had no sooner wondered if maybe it had something to do with Jesus, that the earth shook so hard we were knocked off our feet and thrown to the floor.

Earthquakes are common to this area, yet I had never felt anything that even came close to what had just happened. The first jolt was only the beginning of what seemed like the end of the world. Everything was shaking so violently that getting back to our feet was impossible. The cries of different animals, mixed with human screams of fear could be heard echoing from the streets outside.

In an earthquake it's safer to be outside. That knowledge caused me to shift my attention to the walls and ceiling. Most of the lamps had been extinguished after falling to the floor and the absence of light, combined with dirt and dust cascading from the ceiling, made seeing any distance nearly impossible. Choking on the dust, I managed to tell everyone to crawl toward the door because getting to our feet was out of the question. To make matters worse, it had begun to thunder. Claps of thunder were shaking the earth with such intensity I couldn't distinguish the earthquake from the thunder.

In my years of fishing I had encountered storms that would scare the life out of most men, sending them to their knees praying, but what we were experiencing at that moment dwarfed any storm I'd ever seen.

With the onset of lightning and rain, the decision to head outside suddenly was a lot less appealing.

"He's died, you know," Andrew shouted.

Peering through the settling dust, I asked, "Who has died?"

"Jesus, that's who. Peter, do you really have to ask me who?" he said with disgust. In all the pandemonium, my own survival had shoved everything else aside.

Could this really be the result of Jesus dying? If so, he must have truly been the Messiah. The events that had taken place since the night before and the tragedy of the crucifixion at the hands of those callous and merciless men seemed so surreal, not at all like something that could swallow up Israel's promised Messiah. But if, in fact, Jesus was the anointed one and we were seeing the anger of his Father transcending from heaven in the form of catastrophic weather and the upheaval of the earth, how truly powerful must the God of Israel be.

As the earth settled down, the rain continued for

the rest of the evening. Although we were shaken, no one in the house had been injured, but the distant stares and worried looks led me to believe our journey was far from over.

A disciple showed up and informed us that the earthquake had been so violent it had seriously damaged the temple, tearing the sanctuary veil from top to bottom. I wished that I could have seen the faces of those arrogant, self-righteous high priests when their precious temple was crumbling around them. I wondered if they were wise enough to link the death of Jesus to all that had taken place, or if they would just accept it as a coincidence. My guess was the latter. Otherwise, they would have to shoulder the responsibility of what they had done and that was never going to happen.

When I was a boy, a violent storm struck our village one night. The next morning, nearly every fisherman in our village, including my father, woke to find his boat smashed and broken on the beach. I remember watching grown men crying like small children and wander around in circles, desperately searching for the strength to put their boats and lives back together. That was how my father and all the other men fed their families, but in a few hours it was all gone.

A boat was not something you could replace quickly, and our village counted on whatever the men pulled from the sea for survival. The slow recovery took much of my childhood.

What I had just witnessed brought this memory back to life. For with the passing of that storm, like the many village boats, our lives were laid in

TIMOTHY H. GOAD SR.

pieces, brought to ruin at the hands of murderers in sheep's clothing.

Jesus was our boat and our future. We all had ransomed everything we had and climbed in the boat, hoping his kingdom would become a reality, just as Jesus promised. With all we had witnessed during our travels with Jesus, the magnificent miracles and the way he could enthrall a crowd, why would we have had any reason to doubt any promise he made?

How was it possible that a man who seemed to know what anybody was thinking could be unaware of the cruel and ruthless intentions these men held in their hearts? I will admit, I had always expected them to get over their differences with Jesus and see him for the righteous and holy man he was, regardless of whether or not they believed him to be the Messiah.

These were among the many thoughts that paraded through my head as we sat, gathered together and looking to one another for strength. I wondered how difficult it would be to get out of Jerusalem unnoticed and return to our nets, the only thing I knew how to do. It had been more than three years since I had last pulled a net. My hands had gotten soft, but my back was thankful for the rest. Andrew hardly said a word, but every time our eyes met I knew he was having the same thoughts.

It was later that night when Andrew came to me and trying to be as quiet as possible whispered, "We can leave tomorrow after nightfall, putting some distance between us and this nightmare."

"I am with you, my brother," I responded quickly—

too quickly, I realized as the thought of abandoning the rest of my brothers welled up inside me. The group had become my family, yet here I was ready to flee in the darkness of night, leaving them to sort it out on their own. Running, hiding and lying like a coward seemed to have become my first line of defense. Those were character flaws I had worked to avoid most of my life, and I was sickened by a wave of self-disgust. I clenched my jaw and resolved to be a coward no more.

I decided we should discuss our options as a group, so everyone had a voice in the matter and the terms would be agreeable to all. The reason was not so much that everyone got his way, but to ensure everyone had a voice in the outcome. For three years we hadn't worried with decisions; we had looked to Jesus without question. Now everything was dropped in our lap. Not our lap, but mine. A group accustomed to looking to one man for leadership was now looking to me for the answers, and I didn't even know the questions.

Every minute, I expected to wake up and look around at all the others, still fast asleep with the sun rising over the desert, and realize that the recent events were all a nightmare. But that never happened.

CHAPTER 26

THE NEXT DAY WAS THE Sabbath, so very little activity was taking place on the streets. The women in the group wanted to prepare Jesus' body with spices and oils, but due to the Sabbath they were unable to purchase the needed materials. They decided to go to the tomb early the next morning, inviting me and some of the others to come with them.

I remembered someone saying Pilate had placed a small band of Roman guards at the tomb of Jesus, so I quickly declined the offer to go with the women, citing other reasons I needed to stay put, hoping my fear would not be exposed. I couldn't believe it. Not only had they brutally tortured and killed Jesus, but they refused to let him lie in peace.

As every hour passed I searched my memory, trying desperately to remember something in the hours and years of time we had spent with Jesus, something he said that might have prepared us for this moment. Yes, he had referred to his suffering and dying several times, yet I couldn't recall him giving us any instructions on what to do if it did come to pass.

Of course, that really didn't matter now. The worst had happened and Jesus wasn't around to give us any help. The thought of finding our own way scared the life out of me, given that we were in a very hostile area and quite possibly being sought by authorities at that very moment.

"How long do we intend to hide," Matthew asked.

"Well, no one is holding you here against your will," James snapped.

"I don't recall directing my question to you James, but since you have so much to say, why don't you stand up and lay it all out for us?"

"Men, enough of this foolishness," I said. "We are all in this together and if we keep our heads together instead of squabbling like children, surely we'll find an answer. I think our Lord would be most unhappy to find us at odds with one another. If I remember correctly, he told us to love one another."

"The enemy is out there, my friends," I continued, pointing at the door. "If an animal strays from the herd, it is quickly devoured. Let us learn from that and not put one of our own in that position. Yes, the high priests showed extreme boldness in arresting Jesus, but then again, look where they grabbed him. Not in the temple during the light of day, surrounded by his followers and admirers, but rather on the Mount of Olives under the cover of darkness."

"Cowards, the whole lot of them," Phillip stood up, clenching his fists.

"My point exactly, Phillip," Matthew said. "How are we any different than they are? We are cowering in this room, afraid of our own shadows."

I couldn't help butting in. "Matthew, this is very different. We are the hunted, and they were the hunters. I don't see us as cowards for trying to stay alive. As a matter of fact I am quite sure Jesus would want us to stay alive. How else can his story be told?"

Brother Andrew piped up, "That may be true Peter, but as Matthew has so eloquently pointed out, we'll never accomplish anything hiding out in this room."

Jesus had been dead for less than a day, yet listening to that group one would have thought we had been in that room for months.

"Is there anyone among us who thinks we should be out and about as if nothing has happened? If so, please stand up and speak your piece; otherwise, let us quietly and calmly discuss our options," I insisted.

At least we have some options. Poor Jesus was swept up in a torrent of anger and hate, dying for absolutely nothing. If a man can live that pure of a life and end up nailed to a cross, imagine what awaits the rest of us.

"Peter, do you still believe he was the Christ," John asked in a voice that was barely audible.

"John, I don't know what I believe! How could God allow such a thing to befall his son or for that matter, anybody as kind and gentle as Jesus was? I'll tell you what I do believe: Jesus could have avoided this whole despicable mess had he listened to me. I told him the Mount of Olives was a bad choice, especially knowing Judas was out betraying him. Why, that would be the first place he would tell them to look!"

I had said that already; it was as if Jesus not only knew what was going to befall him last night, but he was determined to see that it happened. I knew everyone in that room, including myself, was filled with anxiety and fear for our lives and for our future. My gut feeling was that we should remain there a few days allowing things to return to normal before anyone left the group and set out on their own.

All at once, a usually quiet John shouted, "So all these past years were for absolutely nothing; is that what you're saying, Peter? Well, I'm not buying it!"

"That's exactly how I feel," James chimed in.

My frustration level had reached a boiling point and I lashed out, "No, that is not what I am saying, John! There is a world of difference between admitting to not understanding what has taken place and saying it was all for nothing."

I wanted everyone in that room to be perfectly clear on one thing; I only knew what had taken place, not why it happened or what we were supposed to do now. I asked them, "If anyone in this room has the ability to stand before us and clearly outline why this senseless murder has taken place and what we should do to continue on, please step forward and enlighten us all." As everyone started to assess our situation as a group, not just individuals, the room fell silent.

As we talked things over, going back over the last few days with Jesus, different disciples recalled several things he had said that had slipped our minds. Most notably were some things he said at the Passover meal.

"All of you will have your faith shaken, for it is written: 'I will strike the shepherd, and the sheep will be dispersed.' But after I have been raised up, I shall go before you to Galilee." I remembered those words very clearly. That's when he told me I would deny him three times, which I most certainly did.

Jesus also said, "In a little while the world will no longer see me, but you will see me, because I live and you will also live. Do not let your hearts be troubled or afraid. You heard me tell you, 'I am going away and I will come back to you.' And now I have told you this before it happens, so that when it happens you may believe."

We all agreed that, in a different setting those words really didn't sink in, but now that Jesus had indeed gone away, could we really expect to see him again?

Thomas spoke up, "He said he would not leave us orphans. I definitely recall that."

"I have to say, I feel a little like an orphan right now," my brother added.

Mary, Jesus' mother, reminded us about his promise to send an advocate, the Holy Spirit, who would teach us everything, reminding us of everything he had told us.

"Yes, mother, I remember that," I nodded. "And think I speak for the entire group when I say the spirit can't come too soon."

CHAPTER 27

THE WOMEN WERE UP BEFORE the sun the next day, gathering their spices, oils and whatever else they needed to prepare the body of Jesus. Part of me wanted to go with them, to see the Master one last time. The other part wanted to stay out of sight, knowing full well that Jesus' enemies would be watching his tomb, hoping to round up the rest of us.

I knew the women would be safe. The men responsible for killing Jesus would never interfere with the Jewish burial ritual. Even the Roman guards would stay clear while that was going on. They might even lend a hand moving the stone that lay across the tomb entrance.

It seemed as though they had only just left when the early morning air was split with the muffled screams of what sounded like Mary, the mother of James, and others. A chill shot through me just thinking about how much attention could be drawn to where we were hiding. Rushing to the door, I hoped to bring that dangerous screaming to an abrupt end before every legion in Jerusalem descended on us.

I didn't even get to the door before it burst open, giving way to several of the women who had just left.

"He's gone! They've taken his body and we don't

know where they have laid him," their screaming voices overlapped.

"They've taken who?" I asked.

"Jesus!" they answered as one, "They moved his body, Peter!"

I questioned them further, "Are you sure you went to the right tomb. After all, a Roman guard was posted and I know they would not have allowed the body to be taken."

In a much more rational tone of voice, but with a look that put me in my place, Mary from Magdala said, "I was there when the stone was rolled into place and I didn't see you. So to answer your question, yes, we were at the right tomb. The Roman guard said they had been there the entire night, allowing no one to come or go, yet there the tomb stood, with the stone rolled back and empty."

As John listened intently to what the women were telling us, he grabbed my arm and said, "We need to go and see this for ourselves, right now." Without any hesitation he shot out the door, so out I went, trying my best to keep up with a guy many years younger than me.

The tomb where Jesus had been laid was nearly half a mile from where we were staying and it appeared John was going to run all the way. I gave it my best, still John arrived a couple of minutes ahead of me.

When I finally reached the tomb, John was standing at the entrance, gazing into an empty cave.

"The women were right, his body isn't here and I stood here as the tomb was sealed," John said, looking completely puzzled. I scanned the area before entering the tomb; there was no one, not even the Roman guards. Stepping inside, I noticed the burial shroud lying on the ground next to where the body of Jesus would have been placed. The stone slab was stained with blood, indicating exactly where his body had been laid. It looked as if the shroud had just fallen at the feet of someone standing there. As odd as that appeared, what I saw next really startled me.

First of all, if someone was going to steal his body, they certainly would not have removed the shroud, but over in the corner of the tomb was the burial cloth that would have been wrapped around his face. Why was that cloth rolled up and thrown in a separate place?

As with everything else that had taken place over the last few days, I had more questions than answers. I said to John, "There is nothing else we can do at the tomb. Let's go back and tell the others what we found."

As we were leaving, Mary from Magdala arrived. She was frantic with questions, but we could only shake our heads. She sat down beside the entrance and began to weep. Although I didn't have the answers to her questions, deep inside something was telling me her weeping would be short-lived.

The news about Jesus' body had everyone in the house in a noisy discussion, it sounded like the market on the first day of the week.

"Is what the women told us true?" Andrew asked.

"Yes, John and I found it exactly as the women said."

Gathering my thoughts, I took my place in the

center of the room and proceeded to try to put everyone at ease with some kind of acceptable explanation. Try as I might, the whole thing sounded absurd.

I shared some of the things I had seen at the tomb, in hopes we would come to understand what might have taken place. As I shared the evidence, I was interrupted by a rapping on the door. It wasn't the pounding of an uninvited guest. No, there was an excitement to this knock, as if to say, "Hurry, let me in for I have something important to say."

Quickly one of the others opened the door and Mary from Magdala hurried in. Her face was radiant as she stammered in her excitement to say what was on her mind.

"It's all right Mary, sit down and calm yourself," John said, leading her by the hand.

"I have seen him. He is alive," she said with hurried breath as she pulled away from John.

"Who's alive and whom did you see," I asked.

"Our Lord!" came her answer.

"Mary, you are grieving, which has allowed your mind to play tricks on you," I replied, trying to console her.

Many times over the years I have heard people say they have seen dead friends and relatives, sometimes even claiming to have spoken to them. Generally this can be explained away due to the extreme distress and grief they are experiencing. After someone close to us has passed, we desperately want to say the things to them we never said while they were living, so the mind steps in and solves the problem.

"Peter, what I saw was not in my head. He is alive and he spoke to me. I even touched him!" Mary said adamantly.

"I don't know, Mary. John and I were there and we didn't see anyone. If Jesus was in fact alive and around the tomb, you would think he would have spoken to us. Maybe you can tell me why he chose to appear to you and not the rest of us."

Mary replied, "I can't speak for our Lord, I don't know why he would choose me and not someone else, but why not me, Peter? I stood at the foot of the cross and watched him die. Where were you?"

That cut me to the quick. I fired back, "Well, then, tell us all what he said. You did say he spoke to you, didn't you?"

With the most serious look on her face, she replied, "Yes, he spoke. First, he told me not to touch him for he had not yet ascended to the Father. Then he said, 'Go to my brothers, tell them you have seen me. Tell them I am going to my Father and your Father, to my God and your God. Tell them to go to Galilee and there they will see me.' "

When she had finished telling us what she had seen and heard, Mary turned for the door. Suddenly she spun around and throwing her arms in the air, shouted again in an excited voice, "He's alive! My Lord is alive!"

No sooner had the door closed behind her than everyone starting talking at once; asking me if I believed the incredible story Mary had laid out for us.

"Could her story be any more incredible than what John and I witnessed at the tomb?" I questioned them. At least if Mary's story was true it explained and made sense out of everything we had seen in the tomb and believe me, that made me feel a whole lot better.

"Tomorrow maybe we should leave for Galilee, that way we will be there when Jesus shows up," I suggested, hoping for some feedback.

"Yeah, wouldn't want to keep Mary's dream waiting," came a response from the back.

I quickly let everyone know that sort of sarcastic talk would not be tolerated.

"Come on, Peter, don't tell me you believe that nonsense," James pleaded.

"Oh, but I do. If you had seen what I saw at the tomb, so would you." The evidence that was left behind made no sense at the time, but after hearing what Mary said, I believed.

While Jesus was still with us I rarely paid attention to the time of day, but after his crucifixion, time seemed to be an enemy. However, now we had a new question to deal with. Was our Lord truly alive as Mary had proclaimed, or had she just imagined it all as a way of coping with his death?

I meant what I told the others when I confessed to believing what Mary had said, but convincing the others would certainly prove to be difficult, especially if no other evidence turned up.

Matthew spoke up, "I respect you Peter, but in all fairness I won't believe this tale unless I see Jesus for myself."

The murmurs and nodding in the room let me know the others shared Matthew's doubts and except for maybe John, I probably was on my own.

I addressed them all one more time, posing the question "Did we not all see Jesus raise Lazarus from the dead, not just dead but four days dead in the tomb? Now I ask you, could God not raise Jesus should He wish to do so?"

That question turned on the light, as they all turned to one another and began to talk it over. James was the first to answer me, saying, "Yes, I suppose that could be true, Peter, but just as you asked Mary, why hasn't he appeared to us?"

I quickly told him I hoped that was not the only obstacle between his belief and unbelief.

John was usually quiet and somewhat timid, but he stood and asked a most profound question. "My friends, the issue of whether Jesus is alive or not is indeed important, but has anyone in this room given any thought to what it would mean if he were, in fact, alive?"

Amid all the turmoil that had taken place, causing division among all of us, no one had even considered the ramifications of his being alive. My mind started racing with questions. If they can't even keep him dead, then how will they stop Jesus from establishing his kingdom? Every attempt they make will be futile. After all, they use death as the ultimate fear tactic, but if Jesus is alive the fear of death will carry absolutely no weight.

The somber mood that had gripped us was suddenly lifted. Now the room buzzed with the possibilities of what the future might hold. Regardless of what we felt, we still had no proof that Jesus was alive and that was the one factor that could crush our hopes.

Later that day, after the sun had set we received two visitors who were disciples of Jesus who were heading back to their home in Emmaus. The two men stood in front of us and told us that as they walked along the road they were joined by another man whom they did not recognize, yet he was full of knowledge of the scripture. Since it was late in the day they invited the stranger to have supper with them. They explained, "It was in the breaking of the bread that our eyes were opened and we realized it was the Lord, but in the instant we realized this he vanished from our sight."

The two men continued, "Immediately we left, returning to Jerusalem to tell all of you of this incredible experience."

"Incredible, for sure, but you men are not the only ones claiming to have seen the risen Jesus. Is it possible you were seeing a ghost," I asked them. The one named Cleopas turned and answered, "Does a ghost walk nearly two miles while explaining the scriptures, and then sit down to have supper with us? I should say not. We have returned to tell you we have seen him and he is alive. Believe if you will; that is on you, my brothers."

With that, they dismissed themselves so they could get back and tell the others in their town what they had witnessed.

CHAPTER 28

EVEN THOUGH A NEW CONFIDENCE had started pushing back the terror, the doors were still locked for fear of not only the Romans, but our own Jewish leaders. With the new testimony we were all excited, desperately hoping what we were hearing was true.

Then unexpectedly, as we were reclining, even though the door was locked and bolted, Jesus came and stood in our midst.

"Peace be with you," he said.

I didn't know about everyone else, but I was glad I was already in a reclining position. Men were scurrying about; hiding behind one another amidst whispers of, "It's a ghost."

Again Jesus said, "Peace be with you. Why do all the questions arise in your hearts? Look at the nail marks in my hands and feet and know that it is I. Touch me and see, because a ghost does not have flesh and bones as you can see I have."

Immediately he put out his hands for us to inspect, and while we were looking in amazement he asked, "Do you have anything to eat?" Someone quickly gave him a piece of cooked fish and he ate it in front of everyone.

As overjoyed as I was, I was fighting back

feelings of shame and guilt. While I had managed to suppress the shame associated with denying I even knew Jesus that night, now it all flooded back. Here Jesus stood, knowing full well what I had done to him and I couldn't even look him in the eye. Knowing the man you dishonored is dead doesn't lessen the crime, but knowing you don't have to face him is a lot easier on the conscience.

Somehow I managed to crawl to his feet. As I reached out and touched them, he reached down and helped me to my feet. He looked at me with such compassion that I knew he was aware of what was in my heart. He said, "I forgive you, peace be with you."

When he had said that, he breathed on all of us saying, "Receive the holy Spirit. Whose sins you forgive, they are forgiven them and whose sins you retain, they are retained."

I was still in a state of shock, first because he had appeared so suddenly and unexpectedly and second, but more importantly, because he had forgiven me for my cowardly and despicable deeds. It felt as if a giant weight had been lifted off my neck and shoulders, allowing me for the first time since his arrest to feel good about my friendship with Jesus.

Not only did he show himself to us, but he opened our minds to understand the scriptures and their meaning.

Just as quickly as he had arrived he vanished from our sight, reminding me of what the two men from Emmaus had told us. He was alive, truly alive, not just in name or spirit, but he had a body.

The way Jesus said "peace be with you," reminded me of the time we encountered a terrible storm out on the lake. The intensity of the storm had everyone, including me, afraid the boat would break up or capsize in the pounding waves, leaving us all to perish beneath the turbulent water.

As I desperately struggled to keep the boat headed into the wind, I happened to glance to the stern of boat, and there amid all that lightning, thunder and impending doom lay Jesus fast asleep. I remember thinking, how could anyone sleep during such a storm? In a flash I was shaking Jesus, begging him to wake up and save us.

"My Lord, how can you sleep as we struggle to save ourselves and the boat," I yelled.

He woke, stood up and said, "Why are you terrified, oh you of little faith?" Then he stretched forth his hand and commanded the sea and wind to be still. Everything immediately calmed down.

The others in the boat murmured among themselves, asking, "Who is this man, that even the wind and sea obey his command?"

That happened early on in our journey with Jesus, before we had seen many of the remarkable things he would do. For many of us, it marked the time we first seriously questioned who this man Jesus really was.

After Jesus disappeared from our sight, I don't think anyone slept at all that night. Unfortunately, one of the eleven wasn't present when Jesus appeared to us. Thomas wasn't there and he refused to believe us when we told him what had happened. Thomas stubbornly said, "I won't believe he is alive until I put my finger in the nail marks in his hands and my hand into his side!"

"I can't wait to see your face when that time finally comes," Andrew chided him.

I asked Thomas why he had trouble believing that Jesus had appeared to us, as if we would make up a story of such magnitude.

"Maybe I just don't want to be misled or worse yet, made a fool," he said.

"I could understand one man not believing another, but a whole room full of people, all seeing the same thing, I think maybe you have already made yourself the fool," I told him. "Either we are all crazy or our Lord Jesus was here. It's that simple." I didn't think he had the right to insinuate we were all either crazy or liars and I wanted Thomas to know exactly where he stood, at least with me.

It wasn't unusual for Thomas to doubt things. As far as he was concerned, if he couldn't touch, see or feel something, it probably wasn't real. While everyone was free to believe whatever they wished, his skepticism seemed to question the rest of us and our credibility and this was something I was not prepared to tolerate, especially when one of those men was me.

On the heels of that thought, I remembered how credible I was. I knew Jesus had forgiven me, but when a man lies in front of everyone just as I did, he should never again use the word *credible* when referring to himself. I believed those days were behind me, never to be revisited, but I never wanted to lose sight of how very weak a person can be if put in the right circumstance.

My father used to say, "A man only gets a couple of chances in his life to really show the man he is inside." I hoped I'd get another chance.

Because Jesus had opened our minds, I now understood what the scriptures were saying, something I never grasped in all those years I spent with Jesus. He had to explain every little thing, not just to me but to all of us. Now we were able to converse with a greater understanding than the scribes.

I knew Thomas would eventually get his wish, but I couldn't help feeling a little sad while he watched in amazement as the group's new knowledge completely baffled him. At one point Andrew couldn't help himself, saying, "Thomas, I guess we're all pulling your leg. We really don't know what we are talking about."

Thomas stood and pleaded his case. "I can see that there is a change in everyone, but simply learning scripture doesn't mean Jesus has risen from the dead or that he appeared to all of you in this room. Why does everyone have a problem with me wanting to see him for myself? After all, I remember everyone in this room thinking Mary was crazy when she told us she had seen the Master."

I could see where Thomas was coming from, so I told him, "Point well taken, Thomas, I am certain you will get your proof and cease your disbelief."

For me, the brief time Jesus was with us, however long it actually was, made me whole again. A new hope had started to bring the freshness of spring to my soul, giving me the energy of a man half my age. I now knew that Jesus definitely had a plan for us to continue on our journey. I hoped he was planning to lead the way.

Jesus left the upper room after his first appearance to us without using the door and without a promise of returning; however, we knew he would and we expected him at any moment. Of all the miracles I witnessed while in his company, his ability to come and go through walls and locked doors with a body I had touched and felt, left me begging to cross over the threshold along with him and be where he was more than any other.

Thomas did not have to wait long for the proof he so desperately wanted. One week later, on the first day of the week while we were again breaking bread, although the doors were locked, Jesus appeared to us just as he had the prior week.

"Peace be with you," he said. Then he looked at Thomas and said, "Put your finger into the nail marks in my hands, place your hand in my side, and do not be unbelieving but believe."

Thomas never even moved from where he was standing. Rather, he fell to his knees saying, "My Lord and my God."

Jesus replied, "Have you come to believe because you have seen me? Blessed are those who have not seen and yet believe."

Then he ordered us to stay in the city until we received the Holy Spirit, or the advocate as Jesus called him. Jesus said, "Once you are clothed with the power from on high you will preach all that I have taught you to the ends of the earth." Then he vanished from our sight.

It's hard to put into words the feeling that had

been rekindled, not only in me but in every one of us. Hope is the one thing without which nothing can be accomplished. In the days following his crucifixion I was at the point of despair, with fear being my motivating force. Fear that we might all be arrested and crucified. Fear of what to do next and of not being able to get out of Jerusalem without being noticed.

However, the last thing any of us expected to occur had happened. Not one of us had even remotely considered the possibility of Jesus rising from the dead, despite the fact that he had told us several times exactly what he was going to do. It was sad that none of us heard with our hearts what our ears refused to believe.

But we could put all that behind us now that our Lord was alive. The first question was whether we would pick up where we left off and shock Jerusalem's temple leaders or simply move on. Jesus had promised us a kingdom where he would reign, and we would all sit on thrones ruling over the twelve tribes of Israel. We began to talk again among ourselves about that becoming a reality.

"With a king that has been raised from the dead, how can we miss?" James said with a smile from ear to ear.

Then Phillip added, "I'd like to see Caiaphas and the rest of the Sanhedrin stop this movement. Why, this will be talked about to the end of the time."

I was sure there was some truth in what they were saying. I just couldn't figure out why we were on hold or why Jesus kept coming and going. I needed him to stay awhile, so all the questions that needed to be asked could be answered. I was definitely seeing things more clearly and with an understanding that far exceeded my earlier years. It was this knowledge that left me feeling that Jesus had something else in store for us.

CHAPTER 29

I WASN'T SURE WHO THE ADVOCATE was that Jesus had promised to send. He had also referred to him as the helper and since Jesus ordered us to stay put until we received him, we were all a little antsy.

Jesus appeared to us many times over the next forty days or so. Then one day he led us up on Mount Olivet where he proceeded to talk about the coming of the Holy Spirit.

John asked him, "Lord, are you at this time going to return the kingdom to Israel?"

Jesus answered, "It is not for you to know the times or seasons that the Father has established by his own authority. But you will receive power when the Holy Spirit comes upon you, and you will be my witnesses in Jerusalem, throughout Judea and Samaria, and to the ends of the earth."

Witnesses? Now I knew why we were spared. Jesus was depending on us to carry his message of the eternal kingdom to everyone who would listen.

As we stood there listening to him, Jesus was carried up into the clouds until he disappeared from our sight. Over the years we had seen him come and go in ways that defied logic, but the sight of him rising into the air and vanishing among the clouds left us standing there gazing skyward with our mouths open.

The silence was broken when two men dressed all in white asked, "Men of Galilee, why are you standing there looking at the sky? This Jesus who has been taken up from you into heaven will return in the same way as you have seen him going into heaven."

With Jesus gone, all we could do was wait for the spirit he had promised.

I no longer expected a new kingdom where Israel would rule. I understood, as did the others, that if his good news was going to be proclaimed throughout the lands, we must be the ones to bring it. I did not know when or where the Holy Spirit would show up. I didn't even know what he looked like, but he couldn't come too soon for me.

We all returned to the same house, and you can imagine the conversations that took place.

We received word that someone had found the body of Judas hanging from a tree where he had apparently taken his own life. As much hatred as I had for what Judas had done, this deeply saddened me. We all agreed upon a replacement for Judas and we took care of that matter immediately. We prayed that our decision would be the right one, knowing what lay ahead of us.

The temple leaders in Jerusalem still had not gotten over the fact that Jesus' body had vanished. The word on the street was that his followers had taken it. Can you imagine the absurdity of that statement? As if we could just show up at the tomb and take his body away from the Roman guard that had been posted. The thought of that made me laugh, but there were actually people who believed it.

I wondered though, if we not seen Jesus with our own eyes and known the truth would we have been among the foolish, believing the body had been stolen? You certainly could have made a case against us that first day.

It turned out we didn't have to wait long for the spirit Jesus promised. It was early in the day, while we were praying. Without warning there came a sound like a driving wind that precedes a strong storm, only louder. Yet there wasn't a cloud in the sky. The sound seemed to descend on the upper room where we were gathered. Some of the men began to panic and I'll admit it caught me off guard, but as fast as it came I knew just as quickly what it was.

You would think that a spirit would come more quietly. We could hear the voices of strangers in the street who heard the sound of the wind and wondered what it meant.

We all regained our calm and moved to the center of the room. Then there appeared what looked like a flame from a large lamp suspended in the air. Suddenly it divided into equal parts and came to rest on our heads. Obviously I couldn't see the one above my head, so I assumed what I saw happening to the others was also happening to me.

It felt as though liquid fire was being poured through a hole in my skull and running directly into my heart causing it to course through my veins. It was as if knowledge were suddenly transformed into a molten liquid, permeating not only my brain but every part of my body. Instantly, I had a large fire of knowledge burning inside of me, not only consuming me but wanting to get out and ignite every soul I met.

Within minutes, we left the house and found ourselves among a crowd consisting of hundreds of men from every country and land you could imagine. They had gathered outside the house where we were staying, apparently drawn there by the curiosity of what they had heard.

I was still trying to come to grips with the indescribable feeling I had and how I would put it to use when I heard the most amazing thing. Phillip and James were each preaching the things Jesus had taught us. However, they were each speaking to a different group, not in our language, but rather in the native tongue of those men.

As miraculous as I found their ability to speak in other tongues to be, I understood what they were saying. That meant in the last half hour, through the help of the Holy Spirit I had learned several new languages. And it wasn't only Phillip and James; all of the apostles were speaking to men who had come from as far away as Rome, Egypt and everywhere in between.

This was God showing everyone there that with Him anything is possible.

The situation did not go without notice, either by those strangers or by the Jewish faithful. As for most of the foreigners, they could not understand how each one of them heard us in their own native language, because we were all Galileans.

The local Jews saw it differently.

"They are all drunk, full of new wine," they wagged their heads mockingly.

What they were saying not only didn't make sense, it was plain foolishness. How could drinking wine, no matter what the vintage or amount, give a man the ability to speak in other languages? Clearly it wouldn't, so I felt it was time for me to set some things straight.

Climbing on top of a low stone wall I addressed everyone within hearing, making it clear that what they were saying was nonsense.

I told everyone listening, "These men are not drunk; it is barely nine o'clock in the morning. No, this is a sign from God, exactly what was spoken through the prophet Joel."

That scared me. I had never read the particular scripture that I had just cited, but there it was in my head, as detailed as a sunset. As I continued to preach, more and more of the men, who were at first very suspicious, had now taken a seat and were listening with intense curiosity. At one point a very large and powerful man from a land I could not identify stood among the large crowd and although most could not understand his words, it was very clear he wanted to hear what we had to say and was prepared to quiet anyone who tried to deprive him of the opportunity.

This journey was only beginning, and already I could see the hunger for the truth radiating in these men's eyes. Even though we were surrounded by hundreds of men, I couldn't help but think back to that first day on the bank of the sea of Galilee when Jesus said he would make us fishers of men. Now, here we were, casting our nets of truth in the sea of humanity with a real chance for an unbelievable catch.

Several thousand men were baptized that day, wanting to claim their piece of eternity. Not bad for our first try, I thought to myself as I looked over my shoulder, hoping to catch a glimpse of Jesus in the distance, giving me a nod of approval.

CHAPTER 30

WHAT IS IT THAT MAKES men hate for no reason, simply because someone doesn't subscribe to their beliefs or perhaps has something new to share with them? Right or wrong, men should be able to live and practice their own beliefs and ideas without the fear of an early death brought about by men masquerading as righteous leaders.

It is incredible to admit that Andrew and I were brought before the Sanhedrin and told, point blank, "You will not teach or speak in the name of Jesus!" Why, they even had us flogged, never knowing how alive it made me feel to be suffering for Jesus.

Well, much to the chagrin of the all the leaders sitting in judgment that day, the first thing my brother and I did was begin preaching the moment there were ears to hear. We had gathered together with the others and were praying to God, asking for the boldness it would take to continue on the path Jesus forged for us. While we were praying, the whole room shook and suddenly everyone there was filled with the same Holy Spirit that had come to us, except this time there was no fire.

Although there was no fire in the air the fire in their hearts more than made up for it, leaving little doubt that everyone would one day hear the good news. Whether they accepted it or not would be up to them.

This community of followers grew at an astonishing rate, which made the Jewish leaders very uncomfortable. They were particularly irritated by the miraculous healings performed daily by all of us. It became almost as difficult for the twelve of us to move about as it had been when the Master was with us.

I can remember one time in the town of Joppa where I was summoned to a house where a little girl had died. As I entered the house I was greeted by weeping women and then taken upstairs to where she lay. As I knelt down beside her, I could not help but think of the time Jesus raised a little girl from the dead. The setting was almost exactly the same, with one exception: at that time we were merely spectators to the greatest miracle any of us had ever seen. Now it was up to me to bring this little girl back. It was at that moment that I came to understand that nothing was up to me and that God the Father, through the intercession of Jesus, would ultimately restore life to that little girl, if that was his will.

So there I was, attempting to do the very same thing Jesus did. After praying to the Father, I told the little girl to rise up in the name of Jesus. Instantly she opened her eyes and got up, and I wasn't the least bit surprised. That's how far my faith journey had taken me, from watching Jesus and being shocked to expecting everything I asked for in his name.

As time passed, my brother and the other ten slowly moved on to other towns and cities in distant lands to ensure that the message Jesus left under our care was preached to every human being. This was a role we all took very seriously, never passing a town or village without stopping to spread the good news. The number of people being baptized in the faith of Jesus the Christ was multiplying so quickly, you could scarcely go to a town without finding Christians.

Christian was a name given to one who followed Jesus and his teachings. The first time I heard it, it filled me with joy to realize I had gone from being a coward who denied Christ to a man who wore the name of Christ proudly.

The conversions to believers in Christ knew no bounds. One of the most ruthless persecutors of Christians, Saul of Tarsus, was himself struck from his horse and blinded by the light of Christ, which led to his conversion to the faith a few days later. Now known as Paul, he is one of the most enthusiastic believers to ever be labeled a Christian. His passionate preaching of the word, with total disregard for his own safety, is unparalleled and probably responsible for more converts than all of us put together.

As I speak to you now, my brother Paul is in Rome to defend himself before Caesar against charges brought against him by our own people. I have no reason to believe any harm will come to him, as he is most capable of speaking on matters of Jesus on his own behalf.

The path we all chose to accept is in its own right difficult, simply because most people refuse to listen and accept the truth, for with truth comes responsibility. Living each day with the understanding that it may be your last or that you may be imprisoned for life really takes a toll on a man. Many days I thought about giving up the fight, but the knowledge and promises of what awaits all Jesus' followers after death is more than enough to keep me going.

One of the hardest things is receiving news about a fellow brother or disciple being put to death for simply following Christ. I remember King Herod arresting my brother disciple James and mercilessly put him to death during Passover. James' execution apparently brought so much pleasure to the Jewish people that Herod had me arrested, with similar intentions I would suspect.

But God the Father had other plans, as I slept while heavily chained, amidst several soldiers with more soldiers on guard outside the cell, an angel of God appeared to me. Instantly the chains fell from my wrists and the angel told me to get dressed and follow him. As we made our way past the sleeping soldiers I remember thinking what a fantastic dream this was. We came upon a large iron gate that led out of the city, which opened on its own and gave us an escape route.

Then the angel was gone, leaving me alone. It took a few moments to come to the realization that I wasn't having a dream, that indeed I had just walked by all those guards and out of Herod's prison. The first thing I thought of was how good our God was to rescue me from these evil men. The second thing was what in the world would Herod think when his soldiers told him I had just vanished in the night. I couldn't help but smile.

CHAPTER 31

I FINALLY ENDED UP HERE IN Rome to preach the gospel of Jesus. It has been three decades since Jesus was crucified, and I wonder if we have been the fishers of men Jesus wanted. To date, maybe a hundred thousand or more have been baptized in the name of Jesus, with more converting every day. I pray daily that bolder and stronger men will step forward to carry the torch of Christian faith after we elders are martyred or die of old age.

Gaining converts in the city of Rome is difficult, at best, due to the ongoing persecution of Caesar Nero. When the great fire broke out here in Rome, he blamed zealous Christians for setting the blaze. This gave him an even greater excuse to execute as many Christians as he could get his hands on—as if he needed any more reason to carry out the bloodthirsty assault that is a daily routine for Rome.

At night the air is filled with the rank stench of burning flesh as Nero has his soldiers tie fellow Christians to poles, wrapping them in cloth soaked in oil and then setting them ablaze. Human beings set on fire are used to light the streets of Rome. What must Jesus think of such a nation, and how can he expect us to ever convert such barbarians to the love he preached?

The road leading out of town is lined with crosses containing fresh Christians nailed to them every day. I thought this would cause men to question whether or not they should accept this faith, a faith that comes with such a heavy price. Yet I have seen no signs of our Christian faith slowing down.

I received word one day that the Roman soldiers had stepped up their search for the so-called "ring leaders." The thinking was: kill the head and the body will surely follow. And while this is probably true in most cases, the Romans and unbelieving Jews missed their guess on this one. This isn't a cult following, as they want to believe. No, this is a belief in a true and living God, the very same God that delivered their ancestors from slavery and promised them a Messiah. This Messiah was indeed given to them in the man Jesus, but their blindness kept them from seeing the truth.

I knew I was at the top of the list, which meant I should probably move to another town in order to avoid lighting up someone's path. I didn't mind lighting someone's path in life, just not their path home. This seemed like an easy decision, so I let those closest to me know my intentions and told them I would send word of my new location as soon as possible.

Rising early the next day and taking what I could easily carry, I headed out of Rome. Being smart enough not to exit by way of the main road, I slipped out on a less-traveled road. I had walked only a short distance, less than a half mile as a matter of fact, when ahead of me in the distance I saw the figure of a man walking toward me. The rising sun was at his back, obscuring his appearance.

I felt like I had been here before, yet I couldn't recall where. Within moments I could make out his face and I remembered where I had seen it before. It was Jesus approaching me, just as he did that first day on the beach. "My Lord," I said, dropping my bags as I went to my knees.

"Peter, where are you going? Your business is there," Jesus said, pointing back at the city of Rome.

I looked back for a moment before turning to plead my case." But, my Lord, you don't understand, they want to kill me there!"

My words, however, fell on the deafness of the quiet morning, as Jesus had already vanished while I was looking back.

As I picked up my things and headed back to the city, the echo of my last words to Jesus hit me like a slap in the face. *"You don't understand, they want to kill me there."* If anyone understood that feeling it was Jesus, when we had headed into Jerusalem more than three decades earlier he knew exactly what was in store for him, and yet he never wavered.

I was right; within days they broke into my house and arrested me. The arresting soldiers never even asked my name. I am sure there were enough witnesses in Rome who hated the Christian faith who were more than willing to point me out.

My trial, if you want to call it that, was more of a sentencing hearing. In a trial there is a process of determining the truth of the charges levied against the defendant, but not in mine. I was merely informed that I was responsible for perverting men against Rome with false teachings that incited men to act irrationally.

Therefore, in fairness to the citizens of Rome, I would be executed.

Well, if treating others with love and compassion as if they were my own brothers is irrational, then I am guilty as charged.

There would be no appeal, of course. The emperor can have a Christian executed for anything at all, or nothing at all if it pleases him.

I forgave him and was led away to this cell to await the inevitable.

It has been eerie to sit here and think of the similarities between my end and the fate of Jesus. No one else knew that night what was in store for Jesus, but he did. As he sat chained in that prison cell, his knowledge of the atrocities of the next day surely began the torturous process long before the first crack of the whip. One big difference is that my end could come tomorrow, or a year from now, or whenever Caesar got the notion.

CHAPTER 32

I T HAS BEEN ONLY TWO weeks, and my date with fate has arrived. Being taken from my cell has my heart pounding, not so much for fear of losing my life, but with the excitement of being reunited with my friend and Lord, Jesus.

I always knew in my heart there was a real possibility I would end up like this, and here we are. I only hope that the years I spent trying to tell everyone who would listen that Jesus is the way, the truth and the life have been acceptable in his eyes. Given the choice, I would much rather live out my days, possibly dying of old age in my sleep. However, I must accept the fate God has sent my way.

As you have led me to where my end will come, I cannot help but notice a boat in the distance out on the sea. You see, even as I am brought to my final hours, my God has seen fit to lessen the sting of death by allowing me the pleasure of revisiting the sea one last time. I can feel the warm breeze on my face and smell the rain from an approaching storm. I hear the sea birds begging for another meal and see my brother's smile after a good night's catch.

I miss my brother Andrew. I haven't heard from him in quite some time. I hope he is well, and I look forward to the day when I will see him again. I know now, it won't be in this world, but I shall see him again.

Despite the peace my God has given me to face my earthly death, something isn't quite right and I struggle to come to grips with what is troubling me.

Now, I know. I know what it is.

I do not deserve to die the same way my Lord died.

So, I beg you sir, could you please crucify me upside down?

"No way! His last request was to die in this beastly position," Servius asked with a puzzled look.

"I swear this to be true," answered Quintus. "I took over his watch at midnight and this is the story he told me. I know a lot of it seems far-fetched, but have you taken notice of the way these men die? We are talking about horrible, merciless deaths from which they show no retreat. Rather, they greet the opportunity to die for this Jesus more courageously than a soldier does on the battlefield. But these men have a choice, whereas a soldier does not, and yet they march onward to an almost certain death—if not death, a life of hiding to secretly worship this Jesus. And for what reward?

"Even as this man hung upside down, gasping for air while struggling with every fiber in him to get another breath, I heard him forgive me and the others, even asking his God to forget our sins.

"I've been around countless crucifixions, but today I could hear the grinding of the nails against the bones in his hands and feet as he tried to adjust himself in a desperate attempt for some relief. In the midst of all that agony, I could see a light in his eyes, a light we could never extinguish with a cross and nails. There is a spirit in these men that no army can weaken or turn back.

"I tell you, Servius, there is something to this Christ they worship, and I intend to look into this Christian thing and see for myself what gives it life.

"My best guess is he has been dead for nearly a half hour, so I am leaving it up to you when to take him down. When you do take him down, give some thought to the story I have just told you. Then give him the respect a brave man deserves, one who followed in the footsteps of glory."

ACKNOWLEDGMENTS

I wish to thank the following people for their contribution of their own precious time in making this project a success:

Mr. George Thatcher

Mr. & Mrs. George & Joyce Leonard

Mr. John Wetzel

Mr. Robin Lyons

Monsignor James McGough

Mr. Nick Pieri

Mr. Woody Cowart

Mr. Aaron Thompson

I would like to offer a very special thanks to these people who really were instrumental in bringing this book to fruition:

Ms. Marie Harris

Mr. Chris Cowart

Mr. Timothy H. Goad Jr.

Mrs. Terri Goad

Mr. Daniel Goad Sr.

Mrs. Lorraine Goad

OTHER TITLES BY
TIMOTHY H. GOAD, SR.

30 Days to Positive Putting

www.ingramcontent.com/pod-product-compliance
Lightning Source LLC
LaVergne TN
LVHW011156080426
835508LV00007B/446